A Murder in Lemberg

A Murder in Lemberg

POLITICS, RELIGION, AND VIOLENCE

IN MODERN JEWISH HISTORY

Michael Stanislawski

PRINCETON UNIVERSITY PRESS

PRINCETON AND OXFORD

Copyright © 2007 by Princeton University Press
Published by Princeton University Press, 41 William Street,
Princeton, New Jersey 08540
In the United Kingdom: Princeton University Press, 3 Market Place,
Woodstock, Oxfordshire OX20 1SY

Library of Congress Cataloging-in-Publication Data

Stanislawski, Michael, 1952–
A murder in Lemberg : politics, religion, and violence in modern Jewish
history / Michael Stanislawski.
p. cm.
Includes bibliographical references and index.
ISBN-13: 978-0-691-12843-6 (hardcover : alk. paper)
ISBN-10: 0-691-12843-X (hardcover : alk. paper)
1. Jews—Ukraine—L'viv—History—18th century.   2. Jews—Ukraine—
L'viv—History—19th century.   3. Reform Judaism—Ukraine—L'viv—
History—19th century.   4. Jews—Cultural assimilation—Ukraine—L'viv—
History—19th century.   5. Orthodox Judaism—Relations—Nontraditional
Jews—History—19th century.   6. Galicia (Poland and Ukraine)—History—
Uprising, 1848.   7. L'viv (Ukraine)—Ethnic relations.   8. Kohn, Abraham,
1807–1848—Assassination.   I. Title.
DS135.U42L8578 2007
947.7'9—dc22   2006022371

British Library Cataloging-in-Publication Data is available

This book has been composed in
Printed on acid-free paper. ∞
pup.princeton.edu

Printed in the United States of America

1   3   5   7   9   10   8   6   4   2

Contents

A Murder in Lemberg

Introduction

THE ASSASSINATION of Yitshak Rabin on 4 November 1995 sent shockwaves throughout the world, both because of the sheer horror of the event and because it was immediately feared that it might cause a new explosion of violence in the Middle East. The most immediate fear (which I confess feeling myself, watching the events unfold in real time on television) was what would happen if the assassin turned out to be a Palestinian? Within minutes, a huge sigh of relief could be felt everywhere from Jerusalem to Washington, when it was confirmed that the murderer was one Yigal Amir, an Orthodox Israeli Jew who killed the prime minister out of politically and religiously based opposition to his peace plan.

Almost immediately, however, the truth began to sink in within Israel and Jewish communities everywhere else: A Jew had killed the prime minister of Israel! How could this have happened? How could the religious and political divides within Israel have descended to this low? How could a Jew kill another Jew for political and religious reasons?

In the weeks and months that followed, Israel mourned as it had never done before, and Orthodox rabbis and Opposition political figures who had preached that the late prime minister was a traitor began a painful process of self-examination, reassessing their previous pronouncements, pondering as never before the relationship between words and action, theory and reality. The mourning and the self-examination continued, but barely six months after Rabin's murder, his Labor Party lost the elections to the Likud Party, and Benjamin Netanyahu, one of Rabin's sharpest critics, became the new prime minister of Israel.

As a new political reality settled in, and soon a second Intifada broke out, unprecedented violence between Arabs and Jews once again began to dominate the news from the Middle East, just as did the continuing strife between Hindus and Muslims in South Asia and between Catholics and Protestants in Northern Island. Religious warfare seemed once more to be normal, even normative, in the modern world.

And so the question of how a Jew could kill another Jew for political and religious reasons receded into the background. But not for me. The Rabin assassination only gave me added incentive to study in depth an earlier, almost unknown, case of an internal Jewish assassination that had intrigued me for years but about which I was unable to get enough information: the assassination of Rabbi Abraham Kohn, the Reform rabbi of the city of Lemberg, in Austrian Galicia, during the Revolution of 1848. First and foremost, I had for years been fascinated by the largely untold story of non-Orthodox Judaism in Eastern Europe, including substantial figures and institutions that paralleled both Reform and Conservative Judaism. This was a story that needed to be told in its own right, to break the stereotype of East European Jewry and underscore its religious diversity in the nineteenth century—and how much more so because that diversity, and the tensions it created, had led to the murder of one of its leaders out of religious and political motives. But whatever archival material existed would necessarily be in L'viv, the Ukrainian name for the city known in German and Yiddish as Lemberg, as Lwów in Polish, and L'vov in Russian, and that city had been annexed by the Soviet Union in 1939, which meant that its archives, like all others in the USSR, had essentially been closed to researchers in Jewish, Ukrainian, and Polish history and culture, as well as most aspects of Russian history, until the fall of the Soviet Union in 1991. Now, the independent Ukrainian state was beginning to open up its archives to researchers, but what chance was there that the materials I needed would have survived all the wars and disasters that had befallen that part of the world since 1848?

Fortunately, during my years of graduate study I had spent a good deal of time at the Harvard Ukrainian Research Institute, and through old friends who had become leading figures in Ukrainian history both in North America and now, in Ukraine itself, I was able to make contact with the chief archivist of the Central State Historical Archive in L'viv, and he and his staff diligently combed through the records and found the goldmine I had been hoping for: the entire police and court records regarding the assassination of Rabbi Abraham Kohn in September 1848!

And so this book became possible: the story of an extraordinary and largely unknown event in modern Jewish history. On 6 September 1848, Rabbi Abraham Kohn, the Reform rabbi of Lemberg, the capital of Austrian Galicia, was assassinated. Earlier that day, while the family cook was preparing the evening meal, an Orthodox Jew snuck into the Kohn kitchen, pretended to light his cigar on the flame of the stove, and stealthily poured arsenic into the pot of soup simmering on the stovetop. When the family sat down to eat dinner, they consumed the poisoned soup. Quickly they all fell ill, doctors were summoned, but they were able to save only Mrs. Kohn and her older four children: the forty-one-year-old Rabbi Abraham Kohn and his infant daughter Teresa were dead. The local authorities immediately ordered an investigation, and they quickly discovered the alleged assassin, one Abraham Ber Pilpel, who was tried and convicted for the crime, which led to a long and convoluted court appeal that lasted for several years.

This remarkable episode has not quite been a secret until now, although even most professional Jewish historians do not know about it, and there has been an element of a cover-up in some treatments of the story. Thus, probably the most frequently consulted source about the Jewish community of Lemberg or Rabbi Kohn, the *Encyclopedia Judaica,* deliberately and rather shockingly obfuscates the facts, writing, "After Kohn and his son [*sic!*] died from food poisoning, murder was suspected. The authorities ordered an investigation, and the leaders of the Orthodox sector, [Jacob Naphtali Herz] Bernstein and Hirsch Orenstein, were arrested. After a time, both were released for lack of evidence."[1] As we shall see, there was never any doubt in anyone's mind that this was not "food poisoning" but quite clearly an

assassination, and the evidence about the crime was so extensive that the deliberations about its perpetrators and their punishment went on for three years.

This is the first book in any language devoted to this murder
and its investigation, although it builds on a small number of earlier analyses in Polish, German, Hebrew, Yiddish, and English.
These earlier studies, however, got crucial facts of this case wrong,
largely through no fault of their own: The documents necessary to
an accurate and dispassionate account of this assassination and its
aftermath, used here for the first time anywhere were, as already
explained, buried deep in archives hidden from the public for
over fifty years.[2]

To tell this fascinating but extremely complex story, I will have to
weave together several substories into one comprehensible nar-
rative. First, the history of the southern region of historic Poland
and Ukraine known as Galicia in which L'viv is located, and its
extraordinary complicated religious and ethnic makeup, including that of its third largest population, the Jews. Second, the history of the city of L'viv/Lemberg/Lwów/L'vov itself, and then
specifically that of its Jewish community, which became, in the
period under consideration here, not only the largest Jewish
community in Galicia but also in the Austrian Empire as a whole.
As a result of its size, location, and the cultural forces that engulfed it, the Lemberg Jewish community was marked by a fascinating divide not only, as one would expect, between traditional
Orthodox and Hasidic Jews but also between Orthodox Jews and
modernists, the latter themselves divided between "enlighteners" either not particularly concerned about religion, those still
devoted to traditional Judaism, and those supportive of the new
Reform movement, which was still being formed in Germany
and, by extension, in German-influenced Jewish enclaves elsewhere. Moreover, the Lemberg Jewish community was ruled by a
lay leadership that, like communal leaderships everywhere and
at all times, was dominated by the rich, but here the rich, too,
were splintered among many fault lines, both economic and ideological. Next, I must summarize the story of the emergence of

centers of nontraditional Judaism in Eastern Europe, from Riga, Vilnius, and St. Petersburg in the north to Budapest in the south, and then focus on the amazing success story of the Reform Temple of Lemberg, as well as the astonishingly popular school attached to it, which, in the heart of East European Jewry in the 1840s, enrolled almost 750 children—a number that even I, a professional historian of that culture for the past thirty years, did not believe when I first became aware of it! And then the life story of Rabbi Abraham Kohn, a gentle and scholarly man, born in Bohemia to a poor Jewish family who, by dint of hard labor and great intelligence, made his way first to a local gymnasium and thence to Prague, where he attended the famous Charles University and then was ordained as a (traditional) rabbi, before taking up the rabbinic post in the small Austrian alpine town of Hohenems, where he served with great distinction. In Hohenems, he gravitated to the newly emerging Reform tendencies in German-speaking Jewry. Based on his success in Hohenems, he was invited to serve the rapidly growing "progressive" Jewish community of Lemberg, where, as he built up a huge temple and school and was appointed official rabbi of the city by the Austrian authorities, he incurred the wrath of the Orthodox Jews on religious grounds, and the even more extreme enmity of the richest (and also Orthodox) members of the community who made their fortune through administering the tax collection system of the Jewish community—especially the special taxes on kosher meat and on Sabbath and holiday candles incumbent on all Jews. These taxes were opposed by Rabbi Kohn and others, both traditional and modernist, as discriminatory and unfair. The opposition to his religious and political views led, several years before his assassination, to both verbal and physical attacks against Rabbi Kohn and members of his family. As a result of these attacks, he was tempted to leave the city and move to somewhere safer and more congenial to the religious modernism he had come to embrace. But he stayed in Lemberg both because of his loyalty to his congregation and because he soon became frontally involved in the great Revolution of 1848, which engulfed Lemberg as it did so many other cities in Western and

PART ONE

The Murder and Its Background

Galicia and Its Jews, 1772–1848

Galicia, the NE province of Austria, slopes down in terraces on the N. side of the Carpathians and contains many marshy plains. Unprotected toward the N. and N.E., it has late springs, short summers, and severe winters. It is rich in corn, wood, salt, and petroleum, but poor in industries, which are chiefly in the hands of the Jews (770,000 out of a population of 6½ millions) to whom most of the inns, taverns, and shops belong. The horse-dealers and carriage-owners are always Jews. They differ in their dress and the mode of wearing their hair from the other inhabitants, who despise them but are financially dependent on them. Of the other inhabitants, who are almost exclusively Slavonic, about 3,000,000 are Poles, who dwell chiefly in the W. part of Galicia and 2,830,000 are Ruthenians, who occupy the E. part; but Polish is the official and literary language of the whole province. The Ruthenians (Russinians, Russniaks) differ materially from the Poles in language, in religion, and in political views. In culture they are distinctly inferior, their churches and houses, especially in the country districts, are miserably poor and squalid.

—Karl Baedeker, *Austria, Including Hungary, Transylvania, Dalmatia, and Bosnia,* 1900

In 1772, the monarchs of Russia, Prussia, and Austria conspired to destroy the formerly great state that lay between them: the Polish-Lithuanian Commonwealth. In this First Partition of Poland, Russia took the northeastern Lithuanian lands, Prussia the northwestern Posen territory, and Austria the southern and southeastern regions of Poland (the western parts of Ukraine.) The lands under Austrian occupation were officially renamed the "Kingdom of Galicia and Lodomeria"—a typical historical semifiction claiming to "restore" a kingdom that existed in the mists of the Middle Ages—Galicia was at once the largest and the poorest province of the Austrian Habsburg Empire, ruled with tight authority from Vienna from 1772 to 1867, and then until 1914 less strictly as a semiautonomous Polish province of what became the Austro-Hungarian "dual monarchy." Galicia covered some twenty thousand square miles reaching from the outskirts of Warsaw in the north to the border with the Ottoman Empire in the south; it contained approximately 3 million inhabitants in 1772, 4.8 million in 1822 and 5.4 million in 1867. Throughout this period, the two largest populations, of almost equal size, were the ethnic Poles and the "Ruthenians," the local term for what we now call Ukrainians. Most of these Poles and almost all the Ruthenians were serfs, literally owned by their landlords and tied to their lands until their emancipation, as we shall see, in the course of the Revolution of 1848. A smaller, though substantial number of Poles technically were nobles, but they were often as poor as their peasants, scraping alongside them to make a living from the land; and a far smaller number were town dwellers. Third in size, at roughly 11 percent of the population came the Jews, and finally a much smaller population of ethnic Germans, almost all of whom lived in cities and constituted the bulk of the local officialdom of Galicia, whose official language until 1867 was German, and whose official policy, again until 1867, was the spread of German language and culture to the rest of the population.

But in terms of its economic and demographic indices, not to speak of intellectual history, this was a far cry from the western Austrian lands proper, not to speak of what would soon become Germany. One sympathetic British historian of Poland, recalling that Galicia had the highest birthrate, the highest death rate, and the lowest life expectancy of all three partitions, commented that "Galicia was in a worse predicament than Ireland at the start of the potato famine," and that:

> As compared with the standard of living in England [in the late nineteenth century] the average Galician produced only one-quarter of the quantity of basic foodstuffs, ate less than the

one-half of the standard English diet, possessed only one-ninth of the Englishman's propertied wealth, and received barely one-eleventh of the English farmer's return on his land; yet he paid twice as high a proportion of his income in taxes. . . . All available statistics point in the same direction: Galicia could fairly claim to be the poorest province of Europe."[1]

Although this may be an overstatement, the economic situation for most of the population of Galicia through the nineteenth century was dismal, and indeed only grew worse as the century progressed. Especially in its eastern half, more rural and more Ruthenian, social and economic—and even political—conditions were far more akin to those across the border in tsarist Russia than in the richer parts of the Austrian Empire.

But with encouragement from Vienna, from the beginning of the nineteenth century, there did develop in Galicia a small but increasingly important and powerful professional elite—doctors, lawyers, professors, engineers, journalists, writers, pharmacists—joined by a small thriving merchant class to form a numerically weak but socially and economically powerful bourgeoisie. Quite naturally, this bourgeoisie, whether of Jewish, German, or Polish origin, used German as its language of daily life, as well as education and culture, and looked to Vienna as its source of influence and authority—until 1848, when, as we shall see, it was members of the middle classes who led the revolution that at first seemed primed to topple the Habsburg monarchy.

This small German-speaking bourgeoisie is crucial to our story here, as the Jews in its midst constituted the group that brought German-style "liberal" Judaism to Galicia. But they constituted only a tiny part of the overall Jewish population of Galicia, which in the nineteenth century may well have surpassed Russian Jewry in its economic and social squalor. We do not know how many Jews really lived in Galicia at the time of its annexation to Austria, given the uncertainty of the extent to which Jews hid from the census takers, and, even more important, whether women were included in the count. The official number of Jews in Galicia was 150,000 in 1772, 250,000 in 1830, and 333,000 in 1850. Even by this low count, Galician Jews constituted by far the largest number of Jews in the Austrian Empire, whose official number in 1850 was 467,000. Moreover, the rapid increase in Galician Jewry in the century after 1772 was almost entirely due to a high birthrate, even though the infant mortality rate among the Jewish population was more than double that of the non-Jews.[2] The policies of the Austrian state in regard to Galician Jewry were always authoritarian, and often irrational. The empress at the time of the first partition, Maria Theresa, was a far more pious Christian and conservative ruler than her counterpart Catherine II of Russia, and she regarded the Jews acquired along with her seizure of Galicia as "a plague, useful to the state only as a source of profit."[3] Her administration, like its Prussian counterpart, placed restrictions on Jewish marriages, hoping thereby to stem the growth of the Jewish population. The Jews responded merely by marrying in secret, and assiduously avoiding state registration. But they could not avoid the new tax on kosher slaughtering imposed on them by the state, and a later tax on candles used for Sabbath and holidays. These were collected not by the government itself but by Jewish tax-farmers who generally advanced an annually negotiated sum to the authorities and then collected the actual fees in the course of the year, as surcharges on every chicken, cow, or goat slaughtered, or every candle lit. Part of the substantial income resulting from these taxes was turned over to the Jewish community for its communal needs—salaries to rabbis and other officials, upkeep of synagogues, the free school for impoverished children known as the *talmud torah*, cemeteries, and the many charitable and public-welfare agencies and philanthropic societies. But the huge remaining profit remained in the pockets of the tax farmers, who became extraordinarily rich as a result. We can assume that they, and the other traditional leaders of the Jewish community with whom they were closely associated by family and other ties, were not thrilled by the accession as emperor in 1780 of Maria Theresa's son Joseph, who—like his counterparts on the Prussian and Russian thrones—was influenced by the Enlightenment movement, and aimed to "modernize" and rationalize the Austrian state, including its Polish, Ruthenian, and Jewish populations. To the Jews, Joseph II promised the lifting of social and economic restrictions, allowing them the right to own real estate, to enter into all forms of trade and commerce as well as the professions, and to send their children to the newly expanding state school system, from the elementary level to the gymnasiums and universities. The stick to these carrots—hardly a small matter for traditional Jews!—was the requirement that the Jews acquire German surnames; abandon their traditional Yiddish for German, to be used both in their daily lives and in their businesses and educational institutions; be subjected to compulsory military service; have their previous autonomous communal organizations abolished, its duties replaced by state officials; wear modern German garb as opposed to traditional Jewish dress; and be prohibited from owning or managing taverns in the villages—previously a huge part of their economic life.

Most of these reforms came to naught after the death of Joseph II in 1790 and the accession to the throne of his far more conservative sons Leopold II (1790–1792) and especially Frances II (1792–1835), and the overall reactionary response to the outbreak of the French Revolution. In Galicia, most of the restrictions on Jewish economic and marital activities were restored, and they were allowed to pay a special tax to exempt their sons from military service, a fiscal burden they gladly accepted. The most controversial Josephinian reform was, however, retained: to prepare them for state educational institutions, special German-language schools for Jewish children were established, in which Jewish religious subjects were taught hand-in-hand with the German language and the rudiments of "secular" education—arithmetic, history, geography. To set up and run these schools, the government hired a young Bohemian Jew named Herz Homberg, who had successfully founded a modern Jewish school in Trieste and was now sent to the capital of Galicia, Lemberg, to do the same throughout the province. Not surprisingly, the traditional rabbinic and lay authorities strenuously objected to Homberg's efforts, and denounced him to the authorities as an atheist and a revolutionary, and ultimately succeeded in stymying his school project almost entirely. This internal Jewish drama took place against the far more global backdrop of the Napoleonic Wars, during which Austria briefly lost western Galicia to Napoleon's Polish vassal state, the Duchy of Warsaw, and then fought long and hard alongside Russia, Prussia, and Britain to defeat the French emperor and his revolutionary forces threatening all of Europe. After the defeat of Napoleon and the various diplomatic machinations culminating in the Congress of Vienna, Austria was restored to its 1795 borders (except for Cracow, which remained an independent "republic.") The administration of Emperor Frances II essentially restored the status of the Jews to the situation under his grandmother Maria Theresa, except for the new taxes on candles and for exemption from military conscription.

But internally, the Jews of Galicia had undergone two transformative, and contradictory, cultural revolutions largely ignored and if noted, misunderstood, by the Austrian authorities. First and foremost, during the years from 1772 to 1815 Hasidism spread throughout the length and breadth of Galician Jewry, and major Hasidic masters settled and established their courts in Galicia, wielding not only great popular religious support but substantial financial and even political clout, often to the dismay of the non-Hasidic but Orthodox, traditional Jewish rabbinic and lay leadership. Thus, major dynasties were established in the towns of Belz, Nowy Sącz, Sadgora, and many other cities and villages. These Galician versions of Hasidism were generally far more radical than their Polish, and especially Lithuanian, counterparts, in their extreme reliance on popular mysticism based on the magical powers of their *rebbes*, and in their consequent rejection of Talmudic learning as the basis of Judaism.

The growing popularity of Galician Hasidism in turn gave an additional impetus to the spread of its most strident opponents, the adherents of the Jewish Enlightenment movement known as the Haskalah. Put briefly, the Haskalah began in Berlin in the mid-eighteenth century, when the great philosopher Moses Mendelssohn first attempted to meld traditional

Jewish observance and belief with the skeptical rationalism of the European Enlightenment, of which he was a central figure. Mendelssohn was certain that there could be no contradiction whatsoever between Truth as revealed in the divine Scripture and Oral Law of Judaism, and Truth as accessible to human beings through Reason; both after all, shared the same source, the living and eternal God. He based his entire life and his philosophical system on this synthetic premise—a synthesis difficult, if not impossible, to maintain for other Enlightenment thinkers or other traditional Jews. Around him there gathered a group of mostly younger Jewish disciples, often less scrupulously observant than he, who set about plotting a reform of Jewish life based essentially on Enlightenment notions of the good and the just but not (for the vast majority of them) at the expense of unyielding loyalty to Judaism as a system of religious faith and praxis. In the familiar clichés of eighteenth-century thought, the dross simply had to be separated from the chaff, Jewish society had to be "improved" both morally and spiritually, and this was to be effected both by literary and by pedagogical activism. Thus, the first generation of Berlin "*maskilim*"—the Hebrew word for "enlighteners"—founded the first Enlightenment journal in Hebrew and the first modern Jewish school based on the synthesis of what one of them called "the Torah of God" and the "the Torah of Man."

Within a generation, however, the Mendelssohnian and even post-Mendelssohnian Haskalah came to a halt in Berlin, its other major center, Königsberg, and the rest of Prussia. First and foremost, the rationalism of the Enlightenment as a whole was being attacked and rejected by the spread of Romanticism, and Mendelssohn's unmitigated rationalism did not accord with the newly popular emphasis on the nonrational aspects of human existence and creativity—the life of the spirit, as expressed through art, music, poetry, the imagination. Most Romantics also rejected what they regarded as the hyperindividualism and universalism of the Enlighteners, and began to stress not what was common to all human beings (or all men, as they put it in the gendered language of the day) but what was distinct to individual groups, especially to groups joined by linguistic and political ties—what began to be referred to as the nation or *"Volk"* (terms that had many different meanings in the previous centuries). The Jewish enlighteners both joined in and were affected by the spread of these newfangled ideas, and especially by the delight in the new standardized German language that was actually a product of the Enlightenment, but now seemed to be embody a particular German *Volksgeist*. Believing that German-speaking Jews could partake of and contribute to this Volksgeist without any loss to their Judaism, the Hebrew Enlightenment became Germanized, and then petered out altogether, as the Haskalah essentially gave way in Prussia to two different processes: the drive to religious reform in Judaism in accord with Romanticism and German national sentiment; and the opposite notion that Jews could simply meld into German society and German culture without retention of their religious specificity, especially given the failure of the drive for Jewish emancipation in Prussia after the Napoleonic defeat, and the retention of the restrictions and limitations on Jewish social and professional advance.

But the Haskalah as a whole did not die—it simply moved. First, its ideas and ideals found a congenial home in Vienna and in Galicia, and then through northern Prussia and Galicia they crossed over into the Russian Empire, where the Haskalah as a whole ultimately found its most long-lived and greatest success. But for several decades, roughly from the 1790s to the 1830s, the Galician Haskalah was a major force in the intellectual life of the not insubstantial group of Jews who wanted to synthesize Judaism with modern learning, civilization—and, equally important—sought to obtain upward social mobility for themselves and their children. Here, however, they faced a major opponent not extant in the Berlin of Mendelssohn or his successors in Berlin or Königsberg: Hasidism, which the enlighteners reviled as the very embodiment of everything that was sick in traditional Jewish society, and needed to be extirpated in order for the Jews to survive and flourish in the modern age. Thus, the first works of the major Galician Haskalah figures were anti-Hasidic polemics, published both in Hebrew and in Yiddish, which the maskilim despised as a tainted, impure "jargon" but used to reach the broadest masses of traditional Jews. At the same time, the Galician Haskalah, tied intimately to the publishing houses of Vienna, produced substantial and influential Hebrew works in philosophy, poetry, drama, and theology, and like its predecessors in Berlin and Königsberg, founded both literary journals and elementary schools to propagate their worldview. Thus, the first "modern" Galician-Jewish school established by the Jews themselves rather than by Herz Homberg opened in the city of Tarnopol in 1813, followed by others in Brody in 1815 and in Cracow in 1830. These schools used German as their language of instruction but attempted as well to teach the rudiments of Hebrew and of Judaism through specifically produced catechisms and textbooks aimed at Jewish children. As we shall see, in Tarnopol and Brody as well, the modernist Jews established synagogues to meet their religious needs, modeled after the great new synagogues in Vienna and in Prague, if on a smaller scale.

Although Tarnopol, Cracow, and especially Brody remained important centers of the Haskalah and nontraditional Jewish synagogues, the most important center of Jewish modernism in Galicia was Lemberg, and it was there that the largest modern Jewish school and the most successful modern synagogue in Galicia were established. It is then to the history of Lemberg and its Jewish community that we now turn.

Lemberg and Its Jews,

1772–1848

I N AN EXCELLENT recent history of L'viv/Lwów/Lemberg, a prominent local historian wrote that what distinguished his city throughout the centuries "was the starkly multiethnic character of its population. By the second quarter of the sixteenth century the ethnic composition of its population was divided as follows: Poles (38 percent), Ruthenians (24 percent), Germans (8 percent), Jews (8 percent), and Armenians (7 percent). No other city in the [Polish-Lithuanian Commonwealth] or perhaps in all of Europe, could claim five ethnic groups each comprising over 5 percent of the population."[1] Although not disagreeing, the editor of the volume warned, in his contribution, that one must not confuse this multiculturalism with equality among the groups, given the fact that for most of the city's history it was dominated "by one socially and increasingly ethnically distinct group—the Polish Catholics." Rather, he suggested, the appropriate term to describe the religious and ethnic diversity of the city was "multicultural inequality."[2]

This apt characterization continued after the Austrian annexation of Galicia in 1772, when the official count of the residents of its capital, now renamed Lemberg, was 29,500.[3] This number, however, had remained constant for the previous century and a half, testifying to city's economic decline in these years, caused mostly by the decrease in importance of the trans-European overland trade routes in the period of overseas colonization.

Under Polish rule, the city known as Lwów was renowned for its handicrafts and petty trade, but it never expanded in any direction that would enable it to compete with its great rival Cracow to its west. And so, as a famous anecdote has it, when the Austrian emperor Joseph II first visited the city after its annexation, his six-horse coach became trapped in mud in a central but impassable street.[4]

After its annexation, the new Habsburg rulers therefore set about to modernize the city, destroying its decaying fortifications, improving its infrastructure, building new buildings that made it look—at least to its residents—like a little Vienna. This architectural transformation was accompanied by the introduction of German as the language of administration, and of instruction at the newly founded local university. It was only now, under Austrian control, that the city's population began to grow, multiplying tenfold in the century and a half of Austrian rule, reaching 212,000 on the eve of World War I.[5]

Jews began to settle in Lwów even before its formal establishment as a royal city in 1356, and immediately thereafter received here, as in dozens of other towns and cities in Poland and then Poland-Lithuania, their own charters giving them the right to self-rule according to their own, that is, rabbinic law (*halakhah*). This judicial autonomy was limited only in cases of capital punishment, and in regard to disputes with non-Jews, which were to be adjudicated by the king's plenipotentiary, by law a member of the Polish nobility. Although we now know that throughout the medieval and early modern periods, Jews in Poland as elsewhere frequently used Gentile courts to resolve conflicts even among themselves—an action strictly forbidden by rabbinic law—this did not substantially reduce the basic autonomy of the Jewish community, or the fact that the Jews constituted a royally protected "city within a city," or rather two cities, as the Catholic burghers of Lwów proper obtained the right to limit Jewish residence to one area of the city, the southeastern part of the town center, whose main street was for centuries therefore called Żydowska—the Jewish street.[6] Given this restriction, the vast bulk of the city's Jews lived outside its walls, in its so-called Cracow district, which in turn became—in fact, although crucially, not by law—almost exclusively Jewish. Thus, there were formed two separate Jewish communities, one inside and one outside the city, each with its own communal structure and chief rabbis—a situation that lasted until the late eighteenth century, when the two communities were united.

But the judicial autonomy of the Lwów Jewish communities did not come along with economic parity with the Catholic merchants, who had the sole right, guaranteed by the king, to be officially recognized as "burghers"—citizens of the town. It is no accident that in German the same word, *Bürger*, means both citizen and town-dweller; that "burgh" or its analogue "borough" function as they do as suffixes in English-language place names or, in the case of the latter, as a stand-alone synonym for a city, town, or part thereof; nor that the words "civic," "civil," and "civilization" all share the same root, the Latin word for city, *cives*. Until the French Revolution, "citizens" did not mean bearers of equal legal and political status in a nation state, but, as in Lwów, city-dwellers formally recognized by the king or other supreme authority as exclusively possessing the rights of untrammeled mercantile, trading, and artisanal activity within the city walls. And so the fact that the Jews of Lwów were excluded from the burgher-class and its guilds was neither a function of anti-Judaism—other non-Catholics also were excluded from this status—nor at all anomalous or nonnormative. This was the accepted status quo of the premodern state, as the great Jewish historian Salo W. Baron first explained, to much controversy among Jewish audiences, over seventy-five years ago.[7]

But this economic inequality did not always translate, in Lwów or elsewhere, into a subordinate position for the Jewish vis-à-vis the Catholic town dwellers. Thus, already in 1639, the latter protested to the Polish king:

> Now the merchant can no longer ply his trade, nor the artisan
> practice his usual craft, nor the vendor his vending, nor the carter

his wagon-driving—and all this because of the obstruction by the malicious and unbelieving Jewish nation. . . . The Jews control all estates, all trade and commerce, while the Christians are only burdened with taxes and penury. . . . They already have taken control over almost three-fourths of [Lwów], while the Christians are confined to barely a fourth.[8]

This was undoubtedly an exaggeration, but it does serve to exemplify the enmity felt by the privileged Catholic burghers against their Jewish competitors, an enmity that resulted in frequent attacks on Jewish town-dwellers, including the murder of a prominent Lwów rabbi, Mordecai Ashkenazi, in 1636, and a formal complaint lodged by Christians in that year that the Jews had desecrated the Host in a public procession.[9]

Despite popular notions to the contrary, such complaints, and the frequent accusations that Jews committed ritual murder of Christian children, were always rebuffed by the Polish king as well as the Papacy, and even the relationship between the Polish Catholic Church and the Jews was far more complex than previously assumed.[10] Moreover, we cannot generalize from such incidents about the social reality of day-to-day relations between Jews and Christians in places like seventeenth-century Lwów: for example, one stipulation of the minute-book of the Council of Four Lands, the supracommunal parliament of Polish Jewry, relating to Lwów in 1607, stated that "those Jews drinking liquor in Christian taverns shall be disqualified from participation in the life of the synagogue."[11] And, most famously, when Lwów was twice attacked by the Cossack army under Bogdan Chmielnicki in the Uprising of 1648, he demanded that the Jews of the city be handed over to him, as "Jews, as the enemies of Christ and all Christians, shall be taken prisoner by the Cossacks or Muscovites together with all their possessions, children, and wives, and the citizens shall not defend them."[12] But both times the magistrate and the burghers of Lwów refused to hand over the Jews. This was most likely, to quote the Hebrew cliché, not out of love of Mordecai (i.e., the Jews), but out of hatred of Haman (Chmielnicki and the Cossack forces) but still demonstrates the utter complexity of the relationship between the Polish burghers and their Jewish neighbors in the early modern period.

But it was the Polish king's support and protection that was most crucial to the survival, and indeed, flourishing of the Jewish communities throughout Poland-Lithuania, including Lwów. Thus, during the Polish-Lithuanian period, Lwów, like several other cities in the Polish-Lithuanian Commonwealth, flourished as a religious, cultural, and printing center for its Jewish (as well as its Polish and Ruthenian) populations. This was largely due to the establishment of Lwów as a major site of rabbinic learning and Hebrew printing, and thus to its fame within the Jewish world as one of the *"arim ve-imahot be-yisrael"*—one of the great "mother cities" of Judaism. The rabbis of Lwów thus constitute a veritable "Who's Who" of rabbinic giants for over half a millennium, including Rabbi Kalman of Worms, the teacher of the greatest Polish rabbi of the early modern period, Rabbi Moses Isserles of Cracow (the Remo); Rabbi David ben Samuel ha-Levi (1586–1667) , the author of the *"Turei zahav,"* one of the most authoritative commentaries on the code of Jewish law coauthored by Isserles; and Rabbi Zvi Hirsch ben Jacob Ashkenazi (1658–1718), also known as the "Hakham Zvi," the father of Rabbi Jacob Emden.[13]

Indeed, it was the Lwów Rabbi Haim ben Simhah Rappoport who, in 1759, led the rabbinic delegation in a historic dispute in Lwów with the Frankists, the radical messianic sect that persisted in the belief in the false messiah Sabbetai Zevi and in a man they worshipped as his successor as savior of the Jews, Jacob Frank. When, to the dismay of the local Catholic bishop, Rabbi Rappoport and his colleagues appeared victorious in this dispute, the supporters of Frank resorted to a tactic unique and infamous in the annals of Jewish history: they—although still Jews—affirmed the truth of the blood libel, the calumny that Jews use the blood of Christian children to bake Passover matso. Thereafter, any possible reconciliation with the Jewish community was impossible, and they, along with their master himself, converted to Catholicism.[14]

It is against the backdrop of the persistence of the Sabbatean heresy, both in its overt Frankist and its covert subterranean mode that attracted some of the greatest rabbis of the eighteenth century, that we must understand the initial opposition of the rabbinic leaders of Lwów—and other Polish and Lithuanian cities—to Hasidism, as it arose in the Ukrainian provinces in the late eighteenth century. Initially unsure that the new movement was not yet another illegitimate offspring of the Sabbatean heresy, the rabbinical and lay leaders of Polish, and especially Lithuanian, Jewries did all they could to stop the new movement in its tracks. Following in the footsteps of their northern and western colleagues, the leaders of the Lwów communities formally excommunicated the Hasidim, banning them from establishing their prayer-houses in the city or its suburbs, declaring the meat slaughtered according to their rules unkosher, and calling on all Jews zealously to fight the Lord's battle against these new heretics.[15] But again as in virtually every other East European Jewish community, Hasidism attracted a good number of supporters in Lwów, attracted by its radical religious and populist mystical teachings, as well as by the less consciously articulated psychological and spiritual security offered by the possibility of following a supreme religious authority in all aspects of life.

In Lwów, the Hasidim split into two groups, those adhering to the more mystical pietism of the radical Galician masters, and those who strove (like the Hasidic movements further to the north headed by the Lubavitch and Karlin rebbes) to synthesize the traditional emphasis on Talmud study with Hasidic mystical practices. In Lwów, the latter were called *"ḥadoshim"*—the new ones, or innovators, and ultimately established their own prayer-house called the *"ḥadoshim shul."*[16]

Very quickly, however, it became apparent to the rabbinic and traditional lay leaders of the Jews of Lemberg (as we move, after 1772, into the Austrian period, I will now switch to the German name of the city) that the greater danger to their way of life, as well as to their power and influence over their flock, came from another direction entirely, those influenced by the Haskalah movement in Germany.

The latter came from two discrete though occasionally over-lapping sources:[17] young intellectuals, usually traditional Talmud students, who, like thousands of thousands of their forebears over the centuries, struggled internally, in secret, and often in great pain, with gnawing theological and existential doubt. Since the Middle Ages, these doubts were addressed and often miti-gated by study of the canonical works of medieval Jewish ra-tionalist philosophers, which at the very least legitimated the existence of doubt, and, equally important, acknowledged the importance of secular knowledge as another source of divinely inspired Truth.[18]

From the 1780s onward, however, there were new answers to these age-old questions: tracts and journals written in or trans-lated into Hebrew by Mendelssohn and his followers, which stressed an even more rationalistic interpretation of Judaism than Maimonides or the other medieval rationalists, and even more frontally demanded that Jews acquire secular knowledge, claim-ing that the ignorance of these by East European Jews was the exception, not the rule, in the annals of Jewish history. Some-times, the young intellectuals so effected were sons (for this early stage of the Haskalah we have information only about men, not women)[19] of wealthy or upper-middle-class fathers who trav-eled or traded with Germany and thus had access to the books published there, or simply wanted their sons to learn the Ger-man language, arithmetic, geography, and so on to advance their business interests. But as we shall see, just as often the wealthy segments of the Jewish community, in Lemberg as else-where, were staunchly traditional Jews who vigorously opposed the new Enlightenment influences hailing from Germany.

But the second source of these fledgling modernists was in-deed the commercial and mercantile elite of Jewish society, which in the early nineteenth century expanded in Lemberg, as else-where in Galicia, to a include a small number of professionals, especially lawyers and doctors. Thus, at the beginning of the nineteenth century there were four Jews among the 320 students at the Law Faculty of Lemberg University, and this number expanded steadily through the next decades, despite a quota system that applied only to this particular part of the university. Soon they were joined by students and then graduates of the other faculties of Lemberg and other universities—philosophy, philology, and, of course, medicine. Throughout the centuries a tiny number of Polish Jews had received medical training in Italy, especially at the University of Padua; now, these were joined by physicians trained in universities throughout the Austrian empire and elsewhere in Europe.

The first purveyors of Enlightenment thought in Lemberg were, however, not doctors or lawyers but a group of *melamdim*— lowly teachers in the traditional Jewish schools of the city, who used Mendelssohn's commentary on the Bible to teach their pupils, and in line with Haskalah pedagogic theory, also taught their charges the rudiments of Hebrew grammar and the German language, and emphasized the Bible as opposed to the Talmud, as the basic font of Jewish wisdom. One of these teachers, Benjamin Zvi Natkish, actually served as a private tutor in the house of the chief rabbi of Lemberg, Rabbi Jacob Orenstein, but he also began to meet in secret with a group of young men eager for enlightenment, several of whom began to compose polemical works attacking traditional Jewish society, and especially Hasidism.[20] Three members of this cell later became noted authors of the Hebrew Haskalah: Judah Leib Pastor, Isaac Erter, and the ultimately far more famous Samuel Yehuda Rappoport, known by his initials as "Shir," who later became the Chief Rabbi of Prague. This circle also included a member of one of the richest and most respected families in Lemberg, Judah Leib Mieses. In a local version of a story that recurred time and time again across the Russian border, yet another member of this group was Joseph Tarler, a rich young man who was forced to move to Lemberg from a smaller outlying town when he was discovered to be the author of a vicious diatribe against one of the most popular Galician Hasidic masters, the Rebbe of Belz. After becoming involved in a counterfeiting scandal with a prominent Polish nobleman, he was caught and sentenced to hard labor, with the proviso— common to Austrian as well as Russian law at the time—that he could be pardoned if he converted to Christianity. Thus, he and his family were baptized as Catholics, whereupon he was appointed the government censor of Hebrew and Yiddish books, and with this power he forbade the publication of any Hasidic works in the Lemberg Hebrew presses. As soon as it was legally possible for him to do so, he recanted his conversion and returned officially to Judaism.[21]

But conversion to Christianity was a rare phenomenon among Jewish modernists, contrary to the impression caused by the examples of Mendelssohn's own children and then of Heinrich Heine.[22] The passionate goal of Jewish modernists—whether doubting Talmud students, secularizing young merchants, university students, or doctors and lawyers already plying their professions—was to forge a Judaism that was intellectually coherent and spiritually satisfying to them. Crucial for them was a form of Judaism that—like that of medieval Spanish Jewry—acknowledged that there was a great deal of worthwhile knowledge in Gentile learning and that the cultural isolation of Jews had to be redressed in order for Judaism to survive. In short, they sought a synthesis of Judaism and Western civilization that strengthened, rather than weakened, the former.

But this was decidedly not the view of the Haskalah on the part of the leaders of East European Judaism, including the chief rabbi of Lemberg, Rabbi Jacob Orenstein, who, after discovering a book by Mendelssohn in his sons' tutor's possession, on 10 May 1816, excommunicated Tarler, as well as his friends Rappoport, Erter, Pastor, and Natkish. (Apparently, he did not dare touch Mieses, given the prominence of his family in Lemberg, including a historic role in the appointment of the city's chief rabbi.) This *herem*—ban of excommunication—was publicly posted on the doors of the great synagogue of Lemberg, forbidding all Jews to have any contact with these young heretics.

But this was Austria in the early nineteenth century, not Poland in the eighteenth, and since the time of Joseph II the Habsburg regime began to restrict the right of all religious denominations to use their traditional policing powers to enforce belief and practice, and hence forbade the Jews from employing excommunication. This was primarily the result of the extension of governmental control over the Jewish community, and the consequent restriction of Jewish legal autonomy. But Joseph had been very much influenced by Enlightenment thought, and there was a vestige here of the Enlightenment axiom, most brilliantly articulated both by Spinoza—the most famous excommunicated Jew in history!—and then by Mendelssohn, that excommunication was in and of itself philosophically incoherent and self-contradictory: It is impossible to force anyone else to believe something, as opposed to acting in a prescribed manner; as a result, neither the rabbis nor the state nor anyone else had the power, and hence the legitimacy, to coerce beliefs, as opposed to actions.[23]

In the event, the Lemberg enlighteners translated Rabbi Orenstein's ban of excommunication into German, and lodged a formal complaint against him to the Austrian authorities, who thereupon forced the rabbi to rescind the ban, and to do so in the main synagogue of Lemberg in a sermon preached in the German language, which also would acknowledge that study of secular subjects was permitted by Jewish law. An anonymous enlightener recalled this event, undoubtedly with much literary exaggeration, in a contemporary letter to a friend that has been preserved: In the presence of the heads of the community, who were required by the authorities to attend the service or else pay a substantial fine, and of a huge crowd that filled the great synagogue of Lemberg and its courtyard to the brim, after the reading of the Torah:

> this Sabbath the authorities brought the great rabbi, our brilliant teacher unmatched in his wisdom, wearing a *tizlik* and bound by two ropes around his neck, in front of the Holy Ark. Here, with shaking hands he took the sermon written by others in German (written in Hebrew characters), and read it out, with his head bent down, his face pallid, and his lips quivering: "In regard to the ban of excommunication issued this summer against the study of foreign languages and especially against four individuals named . . . and on the cities of Brody and Tarnopol that established schools for their children, let it be known that these

bans of excommunication broke the laws of His Majesty, the Emperor, and the laws of the state. Therefore, these bans are rescinded and anyone who issues such again will be punished. And let it also be known that every Jew is required to learn the language of the country in which he lives under its mercy and protection."[24]

This proclamation, the letter writer continued, was then read out again in a loud voice in clear German by the provincial governor Dornfeld, so that anyone who could not hear the rabbi's soft voice would be certain to have heard it now.

This public humiliation did not endear Rabbi Orenstein or his colleagues and supporters to the cause of the modernists, but only increased their ire, and a report circulated in town that some fifty men suspected of Enlightenment tendencies, including Judah Leib Mieses, were forced by the rabbis to divorce their wives.[25]

But it would be misleading to depict the Jews of Lemberg, or any other Eastern European city in the early decades of the nineteenth century, as divided into two groups, the traditionalists and the modernists, for the situation on the ground was far more complex. For the sake of clarity, we can list at least six subgroups of Lemberg Jews:

1. The extreme traditionalists, led by Rabbi Jacob Orenstein, who opposed both Hasidism and the Haskalah, and were prepared to use all means at their disposal to extirpate these groups from Lemberg Jewry. This group included the richest Jews in the city, who made their fortunes through the collection of the special kosher slaughtering and candle taxes incumbent on the Jews, which also depended on control over the official registers of the Jewish population, the so-called metrical books. These men, not surprisingly, therefore steadfastly opposed any changes to the traditional mode of record-keeping and tax collecting in the Jewish community. This group was probably a rather small minority within Lemberg Jewry, although, given its wealth and political clout, disproportionately influential within the community at large.

2. The Hasidim, who opposed the rabbinic establishment of both Lemberg Jewish communities, and often denounced them to the Austrian authorities, especially charging unfairness in the assessment and collection of the taxes incumbent on the Jews. The Hasidim were of course at least as steadfastly opposed to the modernists as Rabbi Orenstein and his supporters, but their primary concern was the legitimization and extension of their presence and influence in the Lemberg Jewish community. We do not have any figures on the numbers of Hasidim in Lemberg, but they, too, were a very small minority of Lemberg Jews in this period.

3. The moderate traditionalists, often but not exclusively engaged in business activities that required, or were aided by, knowledge of the German language and modern bookkeeping techniques. This group—probably the majority of the community—was thus sympathetic to the pedagogic goals of the Haskalah, disapproved of the Hasidim, and supported the abolition of the candle and kosher slaughtering taxes on the Jews, as both unfair and an economic burden. Here as elsewhere in Eastern Europe, these moderate traditionalists were often in practice indistinguishable from the fourth group.

4. The moderate modernists, who openly supported the pedagogic agenda of the Haskalah and the reform of the tax system of the Jewish community, disapproved of the Hasidim as obscurantists, and enthusiastically began to use standard German as their language of daily discourse. This small group encouraged the establishment in Lemberg of a modern Jewish school similar to those in Tarnopol and Brody, and the attendance of Jews at gymnasiums and universities, but did not support any changes to Jewish ritual or synagogue practice.

5. The extreme modernists, who openly called for a thoroughgoing reform of Jewish pedagogic practice, a radical reorganization of the organization of the official Jewish community according to more democratic principles, the immediate abolition of the special Jewish taxes and the removal of control of the registers of the Jewish population from its Orthodox stewards, and the banning of traditional Jewish garb—the long black coat, the special fur hat worn on Sabbaths and holidays especially by

Hasidim, and possibly most controversially, the head-coverings of Jewish women, often bedecked with jewels and other ornaments. The extreme modernists also called for the introduction into Lemberg not only of a modern school but also of a new style synagogue and a modern rabbinical seminary, to train rabbis to serve "progressive" Jewry throughout Galicia. This group, like the "extreme traditionalists," also constituted a tiny number of people within the community at large, but given their wealth and political connections, had an influence out of proportion to their numbers.

6. An unknown number of Jews, mostly but not only poor, who belonged to none of these camps but simply strove to make a living and raise their families as best they could in increasingly trying economic and political circumstances.

To be sure, even these subcategories do not reflect all the real-life permutations and combinations of Lemberg Jewry in this period, or the adjustments made by members of all these groups in cases of exigency. Thus, in 1827 none other than Rabbi Orenstein made use of one of the most famous *maskilim* temporarily resident in Lemberg, Meir Halevi Letteris, a student at the local university, to compose a poem in German marking the death of a powerful local official. More crucially in the long run, the lay head of the official Lemberg Jewish community from 1838, Meir Mintz, though a moderate *maskil* with an excellent command of the German language, was very close with Rabbi Orenstein and the extreme traditionalist camp, and fought mightily against the extreme enlighteners.

Through the 1820s and 1830s, the enlighteners, both moderate and extreme, gained in power and influence not only in the Jewish community of Lemberg but also with government officials both locally and in Vienna. But there was a massive contradiction in the rising alliance between the "progressive" Jews and the Habsburg authorities: as was the case beginning with Moses Mendelssohn and continues to this day, the modernists' religious and cultural agenda was paralleled by a heartfelt commitment to political liberalism. But the Austrian state, run for decades by what was known as the "Metternich system" was, to say the least, hardly well-disposed toward liberalism, and became increasingly authoritarian and indeed reactionary in regard to Galicia after the Polish Uprising of 1830, which was put down with great force by the Russian state but only served to increase support for the Polish nationalist cause in all three partitions. The fight for Polish national freedom was led by Polish nobles both in situ and in emigration—especially in Paris—but also was attracting to its cause the Polish middle class, including the nonnoble intelligentsia.

But not (at least as yet) the "progressive Jews" in Galicia—as opposed to those in Congress Poland or indeed in independent Cracow—who had little or no sympathy for the Polish nationalist cause, and were deeply committed to the German language and German culture. This was so both for pragmatic reasons— they were subjects of a German-speaking state that encouraged the Germanization of the entire population of the empire, a process easier to adapt to for native Yiddish speakers than for other groups—but also out of an ideological, and even spiritual commitment. In line with the Romanticism described in the previous chapter, many modernist Jews deeply identified with German culture as the most advanced bearer of modernity and progress in Europe, if not the world.

As a result, the Habsburg authorities both in Lemberg and in Vienna saw the modernist Jews (and, perhaps even more important, the Ruthenian peasantry) as an important ally in the fight against Polish nationalism, but could not agree to many of the requests for civic equality on the part of the new Jewish intelligentsia, as they smacked of the breaking-down of the ancien regime in France, and thereafter in all the lands conquered by Napoleon, including those of Western Galicia.

Moreover, one of the major demands of the Jewish modernists, the abolition of the special Jewish taxes on kosher slaughtering and on candles, would result in the loss of substantial income to the state. And so, the response of the Austrian authorities to the petitions of the Lemberg Jewish "progressives" was fitful and unpredictable. Thus, for example, in February 1828 Prince Anton

Lovkovitz, the governor of Galicia, met with a delegation of Lemberg *maskilim,* which included the famous radical enlightener Yosef Perl, who lived in the city for a short while, and agreed in principle to the formation of a "Society for the Spread of Useful Industry and Employment among the Jews of Galicia." The leading members of the Jewish intellectual and commercial elite of Lemberg then gathered together a few weeks later to plan the founding and budget of this society, and that June Perl even met with Prince Metternich himself to garner support for this plan. Several years passed with no action, but in time the petition to found this society reached the desk of the emperor, whose major advisors counseled him to approve the idea, as it would be consistent with overall governmental policy by lessening Jewish poverty in Galicia, leading to support for the Austrian regime, and heading off any support for the Polish cause. But the petition then sat on the desk of the emperor, with no action until the Revolution of 1848. By contrast, the regime succumbed to the entreaties of the Jews to rescind the restriction on Jews moving to Lemberg from other cities, towns, and villages, and although it refused to change the ancient restriction of the title and privileges of burghers to Catholics alone, it permitted at least one Lemberg Jew, Mordecai Berish Margolis, to become a member of the mercantile court of the city.[26] Finally, it allowed the Jewish modernists to establish a Jewish orphanage in Lemberg, over the staunch opposition of the traditionalists, but continued to refuse petition after petition about the candle and kosher meat taxes.

Most important, however, the government did agree to a basic reorganization of the Jewish communal leadership in Lemberg, which followed the death of Rabbi Orenstein in 1839. A vote for a new communal executive was set for 1840, and then, given the intense in-fighting within the Jewish community, postponed. After a two-year delay, the government simply appointed a new executive committee, composed entirely of modernists, mostly of the type I have termed "moderate." This group set about putting into effect its decades-long agenda for the reform of the Jewish community of Lemberg. Its first mission was still to convince the authorities to abolish the special taxes on the Jewish population. Its second most pressing goal had been set at a formal meeting even before its members took office, on 4 October 1840: the establishment of a modern, "progressive" synagogue in Lemberg, to be called a temple, with the appointment of a suitable rabbi to serve as its preacher as well as the head of a new school that would be attached to this temple, a "Deutsch-Israelitische Hauptschule"—a German-Jewish elementary school. Letters were sent out to Jewish intellectuals and modernist rabbis throughout the Austrian Empire and beyond its borders to find the right person to lead both these institutions, and very quickly the right man was found: Rabbi Abraham Kohn, then serving as the rabbi of the small Austrian Alpine town of Hohenems.

Before continuing with the arrival of Rabbi Kohn in Lemberg, let us step back and summarize as briefly as possible the story of the spread of non-Orthodox Judaism in Eastern Europe, and then the life story of Rabbi Abraham Kohn before his fateful arrival in 1843 in the capital of Galicia.

A Reform Rabbi in Eastern Europe

ALTHOUGH Reform Judaism began in Germany, developed there both ideologically and institutionally, and had its greatest influence in German-speaking lands, its spread to Eastern Europe has not been sufficiently studied or appreciated.[1] A small part of the problem is simply definitional: it is not at all clear how to distinguish a Reform movement with a capital "R" and "M" from the highly diffuse group of rabbis and laymen dedicated to a modernist reform—with a small "r"—of Judaism, involving aesthetic, liturgical, and theological changes, in the first half of the nineteenth century. Within this group, and the congregations they founded, there was a significant spectrum of opinion on matters both theoretical and practical—a spectrum that roughly parallels that today within non-Orthodox Judaism in the United States, Israel, Western Europe, and, most recently, Eastern Europe as well.

Moreover, most people today quite naturally associate Reform Judaism with its American version, the largest denomination in the largest Jewish community in the world. Yet in the nineteenth and the first half of the twentieth centuries there was, on the whole, a significant difference between the Reform movement in the United States and on the Continent, with the former significantly more radical than the latter.[2] Thus, the introduction of mixed seating of the sexes in prayer services was an American innovation, and only rarely extended to the Continent before the mid-twentieth century.

Today, only the Dohány Street Synagogue in Budapest can give one a sense of non-Orthodox temples in nineteenth-century

Central and Eastern Europe. Visitors to that synagogue often comment that it seems far more akin to Conservative congregations in the United States, particularly in the 1950s and early 1960s when organ music was still common in those synagogues. It is difficult to generalize about "most" European nontraditional temples and synagogues in the nineteenth century, but it seems far to say that the greatest variation existed in the degree to which the prayers continued to be recited in the traditional Hebrew (or Aramaic) original, as opposed to the vernacular. A large number of these congregations accepted what came to be known as the "Vienna Rite," based on the practice introduced in the main synagogue of the Austrian capital by Isaac Noah Mannheimer and the famous cantor and composer Solomon Sulzer in 1826. In this rite, all prayers continued to be in Hebrew, with the exception of the prayer for the government recited in the vernacular, but with the omission of many of the medieval liturgical poems (*piyyutim*) added on the festivals. A central place in the service was reserved for the sermon, delivered in the vernacular, which was definitely not a traditional exegesis of a Talmudic text but a dramatically recited homily, often beginning with the weekly biblical portion but extended widely to refer to current events and controversies and meant to exhort the congregation to spiritual uplift. The rabbi and the cantor wore specially designed clerical garb often reminiscent of that of Christian ministers but with a head covering and a prayer shawl—although the latter was slimmer than the traditional *tallit* and worn around the neck and down the front plait of the clerical robe. The platform from which the prayers were recited and the Torah was read, the *bimah*, was located at the front of the synagogue or at its stage, facing the congregation, rather than in its center and facing the Ark. A confirmation ceremony was held for both boys and girls, usually after the completion of a course of formal study in the basics of Judaism, and meant to assert their conscious pledge of fidelity to Judaism rather than a rite of maturation based on reaching a biological age. Most important, there was an emphasis on decorum, by which was meant that the informality of the traditional Ashkenazic synagogue would be banned: The men and women would remain at their places throughout the service without moving about or engaging in the practice known in Yiddish as *shokeln*—swaying back and forth in prayer; everyone would pray together in unison and usually in silence, with the cantor leading the singing using melodies newly composed by Jewish liturgical composers, with the accompaniment of a male (or often, boys) choir and an organ; talking during the service or the reading of the Torah was strictly forbidden; and the auctioning of aliyot to the Torah was eliminated.[3]

Conventionally, the beginning of the Reform movement is dated back either to the founding of a private synagogue by Israel Jacobson in his home in Cassel, Germany in 1808, or to the establishment of the Hamburg Temple in 1817. In the long term, these were indeed epoch-making events, but at the time they were small local ventures, as were other such prayer-services or temples established throughout Germany in the first decades of the nineteenth century. It is thereafter debatable whether we can speak of an actual Reform "movement" until the convening of three rabbinical conferences, held in Brunswick in 1844, Frankfort-on-Main in 1845, and Breslau in 1846, which consolidated a full-fledged Reform Movement with clear policies and views on matters both theoretical and practical. Indeed, even the existence of a breakaway group can serve as a marker of the formation of a movement: Rabbi Zechariah Frankel, the leader of the more traditional group of rabbis sympathetic to changes in traditional Jewish practice, attended the first rabbinic conference in Brunswick, but objected to the majority's proposals regarding the Hebrew language and the messianic belief, thus leaving the conference and the fledgling movement, ultimately to found the rabbinic seminary in Breslau and Positive-Historical Judaism, the precursor to the Conservative movement.

What is fascinating, however, is that a private congregation similar to that established by Israel Jacobson in 1808 was founded in Warsaw six years earlier! This was the initiative of Isaac Flatau, a former resident of Danzig who moved to the Polish capital for business reasons in 1802 and decided that he could not worship in any of the dozens of traditional houses of worship there, as he desired a synagogue that would be "adapted to the spirit of the age."[4] Flatau's private synagogue, like Jacobson's, was at first meant only for him and his extended family, but after his death in 1806 it was joined by other wealthy and upper-middle-class Jews of Warsaw who desired a "modern" prayer service. Not all of these Jews were of German origin, but because of their attendance at a modern synagogue, their adoption of German-style clothing, and the men's shaving of their beards in accord with contemporary German fashion, they were called "*daytshen*"— German in Yiddish—by their traditionalist opponents, a derogatory appellation that persisted in Warsaw and other Eastern European cities until World War II. Indeed, the Great Synagogue of Warsaw on Tłomackie Street, destroyed by the Nazis after their invasion of September 1939, was called "*di daytshe shil*"—the German synagogue—even though it had switched to having a sermon in Polish, and its reforms were limited to the sermon, a cantor leading a male choir, and decorum. (The Jewish haute-bourgeoisie of Warsaw did, however, drive up to its door on Sabbath and holidays first by horse and buggy and then by automobile.)

We do not know anything certain about the extent of reform in the Flatau service, except that two decades later, in 1838, it was not deemed sufficient by another group of Warsaw Jews, who split from it to create an even more modernized synagogue, arguing among themselves as to how far to go in the direction of liturgical reform. Ultimately, this group settled on the Viennese rite, although without the use of an organ.[5]

Similarly, in Riga, in the northwest of the Russian Empire, a modernized synagogue was founded in 1840, where the Bavarian-born Rabbi Max Lilienthal preached in German to the largely German-speaking Jewish middle classes of that city, and introduced a confirmation ceremony for girls as well as boys. A year later, there was established in Odessa, the southern Ukrainian city already noted for its Jewish heterodoxy, a modern synagogue called the "Brody Shul," as its founders and many of its members were immigrants from the Galician city of Brody; this synagogue was unique in the Russian Empire since it did have an organ, which it used on Sabbaths and holidays. Even in Vilnius, the unofficial home-base of East European Orthodox Judaism, a modern-style synagogue was created for and by the *maskilim* of the city in 1847—the building of that congregation, in what was the middle-class area outside the old city, is the only one that survives to this day. A wonderful anecdote about this synagogue, possibly apocryphal, is that every year after the concluding services on Yom Kippur the founder of the synagogue, the Hebrew writer Abraham Ber Levensohn, would announce "Services next Rosh Hashanah began at 7 pm on the evening of . . ."—humorously testifying to the existence, already in the 1840s, of a significant group of Jews in the "Jerusalem of Lithuania" who attended services only on the three High Holy Days of the year. Later, the main, so-called choral synagogues of St. Petersburg and Moscow, were built essentially according to the Vienna Rite, and other "choral synagogues" were founded in Berdichev, Ekaterinoslav, Kharkov, Kiev, Minsk, Nizhnii Novgorod, and Samara, as well as other cities in the Russian Empire.

In Galicia, as already noted, the first modernist synagogue was founded by Isaac Perl in Tarnopol in 1815, followed by that in Brody. In Lemberg, as we saw in the preceding chapter, such a move was not possible during the lifetime of Rabbi Jacob Orenstein. But quite quickly after his death in 1839, and the consequent reorganization of the communal leadership, a meeting was called on 4 October 1840 to plan the formation of what was already being referred to, in the German style, as a "temple."[6] Twenty-six prominent members of the Lemberg Jewish professional and business elite attended this meeting, chaired by Dr. Jacob Rappoport, and held at the home of the prestigious local attorney, Emanuel Blumenfeld. Immediately the impressive sum of 1,800 złoty was raised to fund the initial stages of the project, and several other preparatory meetings were held before the convocation of the first formal meeting of the prospective temple's board, held three weeks later, on 25 October 1840, at which more than double the original number of attendees were present: fifty-three local physicians, lawyers, businessmen, Jewish police officers, and communal officials, who were listed in the record book of the new temple, which they soon agreed would formally be called the "Deutsch-Israelitisches Bethaus"—the German-Jewish Prayerhouse. At this meeting, the founding group together pledged over 4,000 złoty to fund the purchase of a lot for the new synagogue.[7]

A brief biography of the chair of this group, Dr. Jacob Rappoport, will help illuminate the nature of the supporters of the new temple. Jacob's father, Marek/Mordecai Rappoport, a nephew of Rabbi Haim ben Simhah Rappoport who led the rabbinic dispute against the Frankists in Lemberg in 1759, was—highly unusually for that time and place—both a rabbi and a doctor, and the author of two Hebrew works of popular medicine; his mother Serel, the daughter of the rabbi of Dubno, was the author of a book of women's prayers (*tekhines*), published in Lemberg in 1804. Jacob was born in Uman, Ukraine, in 1772, where his father was serving as town rabbi, but after the partition of Poland the family moved to the Galician side of the border, where Marek received official Austrian certification as a physician, and then served as the official doctor of Kazimierz, the Jewish suburb of Cracow. Jacob was educated both in traditional Judaic and in secular studies before enrolling in the medical faculty of the University of Lemberg, from which he graduated in 1804. By this time, he was already married to Juliana, the daughter of another famous participant in the 1759 dispute with the Frankists, Ber of Bolechów.[8] Jacob quickly established a thriving medical practice, treating Jews and Christians alike, gaining the respect of both communities, and never charged the poor for his services. During the terrible cholera epidemic of 1830, which felled hundreds of residents of Lemberg, he gained enormous respect from the residents of the city and authorities for his unceasing work on behalf of the stricken and their families. His one son, Haim, followed in his grandfather and father's footsteps and became a physician, and all four of Jacob's daughters married doctors, lawyers, or bankers. From the slight evidence we have, Dr. Rappoport's religious views were quite moderate, opposing any changes in the traditional liturgy or the recital of prayers in German (apart, again, for that for the government). He is also reported to have said "We should not be ashamed of our nationality, living as we do among the nations of the earth"—thus ideologically distinguishing himself, and most of his colleagues among the founders of the Lemberg Temple, from the views on national identity shared by most German Reformers—but also, although less well known, by the founder of Modern Orthodoxy in Germany, Samson Raphael Hirsch.[9]

Given the confusion regarding elections to the communal board and its government-sponsored reorganization, the supporters of the temple project did not present a formal proposal to the government for permission to build their synagogue until June 1842. Like many German principalities earlier in the century that were leery of religious modernism as a harbinger, or cover, for liberal politics and therefore often closed down Reform temples after denunciations by Orthodox opponents, the Austrian regime was not certain that it should permit a newfangled synagogue in the capital and largest city of Galicia. But given the political clout of the proponents of the temple, and their reassurance that the need was real and the funds available, the authorities approved the project and permitted the city to sell to the temple board on very favorable terms a lot of 43,600 square feet it owned on the prominent Old Market Square.[10] Soon thereafter, Rappoport, Blumenfeld, and the other leaders of the Jewish community petitioned the government to permit the building of a Jewish school (a "Deutsch-Israelitische Hauptschule") adjacent to the planned new temple, and this, too, was approved by the authorities. The issue was now how to identify a suitable candidate to serve as both the preacher in the new synagogue and the head of the new school, and as noted earlier, letters were sent to authorities throughout the Austrian Empire and beyond its borders to find the right person to lead both these institutions, and very quickly the right man was found: Rabbi Abraham Kohn, then serving as the rabbi of the small Austrian Alpine town of Hohenems.

Abraham Kohn was born in the Bohemian town of Zaluzan on 1 January 1807. His father was one of the few *"Matrikeljuden"*— officially permitted Jewish residents—of the town, but he was desperately poor. Young Abraham was, according to all recollections (tempered of course by his subsequent martyrdom) a brilliant young student, quickly outpacing his tutor in both talmudic and secular studies. The family therefore scraped together enough resources to send the twelve-year-old Abraham to the gymnasium in the nearby town of Pisek, where he excelled as well. His extant record at the Pisek gymnasium is a wonderful piece of evidence of the basic curriculum at a provincial Austrian gymnasium in the early nineteenth century: the courses included Religion, the New Testament, Biblical History, German Literature, Latin Literature, German Calligraphy, Latin Calligraphy, Arithmetic, Grammar, Geography, Geometry, Architecture, Mechanics, Natural History, and Biology. In all of the subjects that were graded, Kohn received the highest grade possible *"sehr gut"* (very good).[11] While he was in Pisek, Kohn's mother died, and his father soon remarried; a son of this second marriage was Bernhard Kohn, later a famous piano manufacturer and Jewish philanthropist in Vienna. A good deal of Abraham Kohn's correspondence with his younger half-brother survives, and serves as invaluable source material about his life, both before and in Lemberg.

From Pisek, Kohn went on to the nearby larger town of Jungbunzlau (known in Czech as Mladá Boleslav), where he received the "Humaniorem" degree, equivalent to some extent to an American M.A. (as graduation from a gymnasium was roughly equivalent to a B.A., and the first degree at European universities was the doctorate). Here he also furthered his Talmudic studies with the well-known local rabbi Isaac Spitz, and supported himself by working as a tutor in the home of one Salomon Neustadl, where, it was reported, he was caught by his employer reading Montesquieu's *Spirit of the Laws* while still clad in *tallit* and *tefillin*, but was saved from being fired as a heretic due to the intervention of Rabbi Spitz, who testified to Kohn's Orthodoxy.[12] Around this time, he received an official certification from the Prague Jewish "Hauptschule" that he was competent to serve as a teacher in any Jewish school in the Austrian Empire. That certificate read: "Abraham Kohn, from Zaluzan, Prachiner Region in Bohemia, has as of this date fulfilled all the requirements to serve as a teacher of the Hebrew language, having mastered all the theoretical and practical skills necessary thereunto."[13] Several years later, he received a general letter of recommendation as a potential teacher in any Jewish school in the Austrian Empire from none other than Herz Homberg, still recognized as an authority by the regime though detested and ignored by the Jews.

It is not clear whether Kohn actually used this diploma and recommendation for any teaching job, since in the meanwhile he had moved on to Prague itself, where he enrolled in the philosophical faculty of the famous Charles University, while studying Talmud with the renowned Chief Rabbi Samuel Landau, famous not only for his learning and his traditionalism but also for his fervent opposition to the Austrian emperor's plan, at the end of the eighteenth century, to establish government-sponsored theological seminaries in the empire. Due to the Kohn family's distressing economic situation, Abraham was forced to abandon his university studies, and so never obtained a doctorate. But he continued his rabbinic training, and on 13 January 1832, in the traditional ceremony of one-on-one *semikhah*, he was ordained as a rabbi by Chief Rabbi Landau: "I, Chief Rabbi [of Prague] hereby testify that Abraham Kohn, from Zaluzan in the Prachiner Region has today been examined by me in both parts of the *Shulhan Arukh, Yore Deah* and *Orah Hayim*, which he has successfully mastered, along with a deep knowledge of rabbinic sources. He therefore possesses all the knowledge and skills necessary to serve as a teacher and rabbi in Israel, and is recommended to all Jewish communities in these capacities. I also testify, in addition to the above, to his irreproachable moral and religious conduct."[14]

In line with the customs of the age, a few months later, Kohn had yet another rabbi, Samuel Kauder, the Chief Rabbi of Kalladey, Bohemia, issue a similar writ of ordination.[15]

It is clear, then, that although his personal level of religious observance and piety and the degree of his Talmudic knowledge would become matters of great controversy later in Lemberg, Kohn was quite a learned Talmudist and an excellent Hebraist, and, at least at the beginning of his career, a fully observant traditional Jew. Despite his credentials, to his great shock and disappointment he did not receive the first rabbinic position he applied for, as District Rabbi of Saaz and Elbogen. But soon another, if lesser, position, opened up, as the rabbi of the Tyrolean town of Hohenems, which contained a Jewish population of only ninety families. Kohn applied for this position, and was invited to give a trial sermon, which he gave there in the summer of 1833.

Interestingly, his main competitor for this position was Rabbi Samuel Holdheim, later one of the most radical reformers in Germany but now also a young rabbi (one year older than Kohn) desperately looking for employment. Holdheim, too, had been ordained by Chief Rabbi Landau of Prague, whose letter of *semikhah* is far more abundant of praise in regard to his Talmudic learning than that of Kohn. It is crucial to underscore that Rabbi Landau was not being naïve in his ordination either of Holdheim or of Kohn: the early Reformers all began life as traditional Jews and only slowly had their religious views evolve in the direction of Reform. Many of this first generation of Reformers, such as Holdheim, Aaron Chorin of Hungary, and especially the most important leader of Reform Judaism in Germany, and arguably in its entire history, Abraham Geiger, were extremely erudite Talmud scholars.

On paper, Holdheim seems to have been a better candidate for the position in Hohenems than Kohn: beyond his rabbinic prowess, he also had a doctorate from the University of Leipzig, and Rabbi Landau's letter of recommendation included the information that Holdheim came from a rich family and was a widower with no children, and therefore, were he chosen, would not need much support from the Jewish community of

Hohenems.[16] But Kohn impressed the leaders of the Hohenems Jewish community more than did his rival, possibly because he was said to be a great preacher, despite his oft-commented-on personal shyness and nervous temperament. A strong recommendation from Cantor Solomon Sulzer, a native of the town, also could not have hurt. And so Abraham Kohn received the offer of the rabbinate of Hohenems, with a three-year renewable contract, and moved to the Alpine town in the fall of 1833.

Soon after arriving there, he met the woman who would be his bride: Magdalena Kahn was the daughter of a well-to-do merchant in the Bavarian town of Fellheim, whose mother came from Hohenems and whose brother had moved there to work for the family business. She brought a substantial dowry to a potential groom, but when she and Rabbi Kohn were married, in 1835, most of the dowry money was retained by her father as an investment in the family business, and the young couple was forced to live on the rather meager salary of a small-town rabbi. At least they soon moved from the tiny rooms in the synagogue provided by the community to larger quarters in the home of Joseph Sulzer, the father of Solomon, which soon accommodated a large family: Jacob, born in 1836, later a lawyer in Galicia and his father's first biographer;[17] Joseph, born in 1838, who also became a lawyer in Galicia; Angelica, born in 1839, who married a man named Hofheimer and emigrated to Brooklyn; and Gotthilf, later a writer in a suburb of Lemberg, and the author of the most substantial biography of his martyred father.[18] (A fifth child, Teresa, would be born in Lemberg in 1847 and die with her father in 1848.)

By all accounts, Rabbi Kohn's decade-long service in Hohenems was very successful. Apart from serving the traditional function of the rabbi as chief halachic arbiter, which included, in the Austrian empire, denouncing to the Austrian authorities any community members who departed from traditional Jewish practice, such as observance of the Sabbath[19]—he reorganized the local burial society, founded a society to train young Jews in artisan handiworks and crafts, and successfully restructured both the local Hebrew school and the classes in Judaism taught in the government school. And he became a highly admired preacher, giving impressive sermons every Saturday and holiday.

The latter functions testify to the changing role of the rabbinate in nineteenth-century Central and Western Europe, soon to be transported not only to America but to the non-Orthodox congregations of Eastern Europe as well: traditionally, communal rabbis served almost exclusively as legal authorities, adjudicating matters of Jewish law for their flock, and generally gave public sermons only twice a year, on the Sabbaths before Passover and Yom Kippur.[20] The new-style rabbis (soon to include both Orthodox, Conservative, and Reform) formally had responsibility for the education of Jewish children from the age of six or seven to adolescence; fulfilled many pastoral functions previously either unknown in the Jewish community or carried out by voluntary associations; and most important, were expected to deliver uplifting sermons every Sabbath and holiday, not simply to preach for the sake of preaching but also to uplift their flock's religious consciousness by means of these dramatic homilies.

Indeed, so successful was Abraham Kohn in the latter role that only a year after he arrived in Hohenems, six of his sermons preached there were published in Prague as a stand-alone book: *Sechs Predigten gehalten in der Synagogue zu Hohenems von dortigen Rabbiner Abraham Kohn* (Six Sermons Delivered in the Synagogue of Hohenems by the local rabbi Abraham Kohn).[21] The titles of these sermons were: "Divine Blessing," given on the Sabbath of "Parshat Ekev"—that is, when the Torah portion was Deuteronomy 7:12–11:25; "Prayer," given on Yom Kippur; "The Strength of Belief," given on the Sabbath of Hanukkah; "The Meaning and Importance of the Sabbath," given on the Sabbath of the Intermediate Days of Passover; "Charity," given on Shabbat Bahar—that is, Leviticus 25:1–26:2; and "Israel, God's Chosen People," given on Shavuot.

It is interesting to speculate why a twenty-seven-year-old rabbi in a small town in rural Austria would decide to have his sermons published at this stage of his career—or why a publisher in Prague would decide to publish them. Clearly, despite his characterization as shy and nervous, there must have been some keen spark of ambition in this young man, and from the publisher's point of view, there must have been a market for such wares. In his introduction, Kohn himself remarked on the latter, noting the lack of suitable reading material on Judaism in German for the intelligent Jew who wants truly to understand his faith. He then raised for the first time what would become one of the salient leitmotifs of this volume, and his career, as a whole: "Our coreligionists sorely lack any knowledge of the essence of our Religion, since their education has either been neglected or perverted, so that the Judaism of so many Jews has become nothing more than a collection of prohibitions, demands, and habits inherited from their fathers, which they obey unselfconsciously and in an unholy manner. They therefore desperately need religious enlightenment, so that they can both observe and understand the Judaism they practice—or ought to practice."[22]

From the start, then, we begin to hear the voice of a rabbi committed to the explication of Judaism in accordance with modern sensibilities. Throughout the volume, no specific "reforms" are advocated, liturgical or ritual. But there is no doubt that the young Hohenems rabbi is here engaged in a critical effort to transform the Judaism not only of his community but of his potential readers as well. Essentially, two themes dominate the sermons: the meaninglessness of material versus spiritual riches, and the necessity to understand that true religiosity consists in sincere inner devotion to God and His teachings, rather than in external performance of empty ceremonies and rituals. The first theme is repeated throughout the homilies, particularly in the sermon stressing the Deuteronomic teaching of attaining God's blessing through working the land and fulfilling His commandments, and in the sermon on charity. Here Kohn rehearses the familiar themes of both the European and the Jewish Enlightenments, that in order to be "normal" the Jews must move away from their traditional almost complete engagement in money-lending and other forms of commerce to engage in artisan crafts and agriculture, and the latter especially for the poor Jews, who were not surviving economically in the transition from the old market economy of pre-nineteenth-century Central Europe to the new precapitalist economy of the Habsburg Empire. In line with the conventional Haskalah trope, he expresses deep gratitude to the Austrian Emperor—"the most gracious father of our country (*unseres huldreichsten Landsvater*)" for abolishing the old restrictions on Jewish economic practices, and urges the Jews to take advantage of this progressive time in their history to mend their ways. However, this Enlightenment lesson is filtered quite clearly through the teachings of early nineteenth-century Romanticism: Although Kohn implicitly cites Montesquieu on the nature of money and the origin of trade,[23] he departs radically from the latter's positive attitude to commercial enterprises, enunciating a decidedly Romantic distaste for the material as opposed to the spiritual, and spends most of the first published sermon extolling the central Romantic theme of the moral superiority of what we now call "bourgeois" marriage and child rearing.

But the second motif actually dominates this small volume: the contemporary situation of the Jews in the Austrian empire is analogous, Kohn repeatedly claims, to that condemned by the prophets of yore. The Jews engage in meaningless ceremonial practices and ritual and think that by this means they are fulfilling the Lord's commands. But they are wrong: as the ancient seers repeatedly, but unsuccessfully, taught the Israelites, God has no interest in ceremonies empty of spirituality, in sacrifices offered by those who are morally and ethically sinful, or in fulfillment of religious duties out of sheer habit, or even out of obeisance to parents' traditions. In his Yom Kippur sermon in particular, he chastises his congregation that what is called a religious (*fromm*) Jew is seriously errant, and even fatal to the future of Judaism and the Jewish people: religiosity consists in obeying both the ethical and the ritual commandments of God, not simply the latter. What is required, once more, is a religious enlightenment of the Jews, effected primarily through education, to lead them back to true Judaism, and thence to God.

Crucial, here, is not only what is said but what is not said in this small book. Contrary to the view already expressed among some Reform thinkers for the last two decades, the Jews are referred to by Kohn as a "nation" and the Land of Israel is repeatedly called "our Fatherland." Only in one sermon can we detect, without anachronistic retrojection, the voice of a reforming rabbi: in his homily on, of all things, Leviticus 25:1–26:2, in which the Israelites are clearly forbidden to take interest from their brethren, Kohn deliberately focuses on the biblical extension of this prohibition to "the stranger and resident who dwell among you," but refrains from making any mention of the elaborate rules of postbiblical Judaism which permit interest-taking from non-Jews, not to speak of the fact that Maimonides himself listed taking interest from non-Jews as one of the positive commandments of Judaism in his own list of *mitzvot*. However, as his son claims in his biography of Abraham Kohn that the Austrian censor intervened very heavily in the last two sermons in the book—this one, on Charity, and the last, on the Chosenness of the Jewish People—perhaps this omission was the result more of the censor's black pen than of Kohn's own sensibilities.

Soon after the publication of *Six Sermons*, Kohn began to work on a second book, a textbook of Hebrew grammar meant for modern Jewish religious schools throughout the German-speaking lands and beyond. At first he could not find a publisher for this work and had it published at his own expense, but then a Jewish publisher from, of all places, Smyrna in the Ottoman Empire, asked for permission to publish a second edition, which was published there in 1841.[24] This was a standard version of a nineteenth-century Haskalah-influenced Hebrew primer, and contained no hint of any further Reform sensibilities, and the same was true of the third and fourth books Kohn published later, a textbook on biblical history that hewed completely to the traditional view of the Bible, and a primer on Judaism for Jewish children.[25]

But Kohn articulated quite different sensibilities in the scholarly articles that he wrote in the burgeoning periodical literature of German-speaking Jewry in the late 1830s, particularly in the 1837–1839 volumes of Abraham Geiger's *Wissenschaftliche*

Zeitschrift für jüdische Theologie (Scholarly Journal for Jewish Theology). These pieces, on Jewish mourning rituals, the custom of not wearing leather on Yom Kippur, music on holy days, and hair-coverings of women, testify to far more radical views on Judaism that we could have expected from the Hohenems homilies.[26]

The first article, on mourning rituals, already indicates Kohn's scholarly methodology and the nature and tone of his overall conclusions. After examining the history of Jewish mourning customs as evidenced in the Bible, the Mishnah, the Talmud, and later codes, he concludes first, that there has obviously been historical development in regard to these customs, and that most of the customs that Jews observe at present are not only postbiblical and hence of lower rabbinic, as opposed to higher scriptural authority, but post-Talmudic, and caused by local circumstances. He therefore denounces as totally lacking sound biblical or Talmudic grounding four customs practiced by Jews in his (and our) day: the tearing of a piece of clothing at a burial; not wearing leather shoes and sitting on the ground or on low stools during the shiva period; and not shaving for thirty days after the burial. These customs, he asserts, were introduced into Judaism not by God in the Bible or by the rabbis in the Mishnah or Talmud, but by folk custom, and specifically the customs of "oriental Jews" whose entire mode of life and surrounding civilization was primitive, and in every possible way different from, and alien to, the *Zeitgeist* of German-speaking Jewry in the nineteenth century. True, these customs are still observed, and considered untouchable, by Polish Jews in his days, but then Polish Jews are not much more advanced in their intellectual or moral development than the "oriental Jews" of the medieval and early modern ages, and are renowned for their backwardness and fanaticism. But "we, as entirely European and as Germans" ("*wir, als vollkommene Europäer, als Deutsche*")[27] find these customs alien and repulsive, and indeed, at times frightening as well. Waxing Montesqueian, he explains that "among us cold-blooded Germans, true pain is deeper and more reserved," and thus all these oriental customs must simply be abolished in order to preserve not only a historically authoritative Judaism but also one in line with the spirit of the ages and true religiosity.

Similarly, his second and third articles review the history of the custom of not wearing leather on Yom Kippur and not playing music on Sabbaths and holidays, finds these customs halachically not binding and inappropriate to modern sensibilities, and calls for their abolition by progressive Jews. And, finally, his last article of the series, on the head-coverings of married women (including, in some cases, the shaving of their heads before marriage) is the most vituperative of the lot: the entire differentiation between the head-coverings of married and unmarried women, he asserts, is not only halachically insupportable but based on a misreading of the sources, and is in fact an imitation of medieval German practice on the part of the Jews—*nicht altjüdische, sondern altdeutsche Sitte* (an old-German rather than old-Jewish custom).[28] Because it is also insulting to the dignity of contemporary Jewish women, it must forthwith be abolished.

We do not have any evidence that in his real life or communal practice Abraham Kohn abolished the three first customs he denounced in these scholarly pieces, although we do know that beginning in Hohenems and continuing in Lemberg, he permitted his wife to wear her own hair uncovered. But on the basis of his ideological and religious beliefs, as expressed in these writings, it is abundantly clear that he belongs to the category of "Reform" rather than merely "nontraditional" rabbis, especially in the Austrian and then Galician contexts in which he lived and work.

Although his son Gotthilf claims that his father's decision to try out for the position of preacher and teacher of the "progressive Jewish community" of Lemberg was the result of a dispute between Rabbi Kohn and a congregant whose son had married a non-Jew, which then the rabbi preached against in the synagogue the next Sabbath, the more authoritative historian of the Jewish community of Hohenems argues that this story is not true, and that Rabbi Kohn was simply bored after a decade in the tiny provincial Alpine town, and was looking for a bigger audience among whom to propound his increasingly radical views.[29]

That he would surely find in the largest Jewish community of the Austrian Empire, but one also right in the heart of that Polish Jewry which Abraham Kohn had condemned as barbaric, primitive, and "oriental." He would soon find out just how receptive these Polish Jews were to his modern views.

Rabbi Abraham Kohn in Lemberg,
1843–1848

Iᴺ ᴛʜᴇ ᴀʀᴄʜɪᴠᴇs of the city of L'viv, one of the first documents relating to Abraham Kohn is the official announcement, dated July 23, 1843 of his trial sermon: "Abraham Kohn, Chief Rabbi of the Jewish community of Hohenems, in the Tyrolean Alps, will preach on Saturday morning, *Parshat Va-ethanan*, between *shaharit* and *musaf*, in the Great Synagogue. The listeners are instructed and required to behave quietly, to sit in their seats during the sermon, and no one should either speak or walk about."[1] Clearly, the leaders of the Jewish community, led by Dr. Jacob Rappoport and Emanuel Blumenfeld, were nervous that the crowd at the traditional main synagogue of the city, located outside the town walls, would not embarrass them before the visiting prospective rabbi, whom they were just as anxious to impress as he was to impress them.

That first sermon took place on Saturday, August 19, 1843.[2] Demonstrating his formidable homiletical skill honed in Hohenems, and repeating themes he had often preached and written about before, Kohn spoke in a clear voice, in standard High German tinged with an Austrian accent. Taking as his proof text Malachi 2:6: "True instruction was in his mouth, and no wrong was found in his lips. He walked in peace and uprightness, and turned away from iniquity," Kohn exhorted his new audience that there were times, and not so long ago, that these words of the Prophet were not heeded in Israel, and false religion was practiced among the Jews. They confused ceremonies followed blindly by rote or pretentious but ultimately empty casuistry with the true teachings of the Torah. But how wonderfully things have changed in the most recent years, when both *"Bildung"* and *"Wissenschaft"*—moral education and scientific scholarly study— have taken hold in Jewish life, and so the possibility now exists for a regeneration of Judaism on their basis, leading to a new enlightened, Judaism, which would in fact be the true Judaism, synthesizing the ceremonial and the ethical laws of God. Despite the difficulties that lie ahead, there is nothing to fear from such a future, he concluded: Truth shall always vanquish Falsehood, and all classes and groups of Jews—men and women, alike—can unite under this banner to seek a Judaism that will lead all of them forward to a better life, under the generous aegis of the gracious emperor and his government.

The leaders of the Jewish community and the temple committee were thrilled by the young rabbi's sermon, by his German, his bearing, his modernist Judaism (that, not incidentally, did not include, or even allude to, the program of abolishing time-honored customs that he had raised in his scholarly articles). Indeed, so impressed were they by the rabbi from Hohenems that they immediately decided to stop the search process and hire him, and on the spot offered him the position in Lemberg, which he then accepted.

The contract signed between the two parties stipulated that as of 1 November 1843, Rabbi Abraham Kohn would assume the position of "teacher of religion" (*Religionsweiser*) and preacher (*Prediger*) in the Lemberg Jewish community, along with all duties and responsibilities assigned thereto by the civil and political laws of the state, including the right of residence in the city. The salary for this position will be 600 Gulden per annum, plus moving, housing and other domestic expenses, and all the benefits that accrue to this office.[3] On completion of the new "German-Jewish Prayer-House," Rabbi Kohn would preach there in German every other Sabbath and on all holidays, and perform all other duties incumbent on the rabbi of such a temple, such as confirmation of the youth. He would take control of the women's association, the association for Jewish orphans and the home for

foster children, and supervise their moral and religious training. Without offending the conscience of "certain members" of
our community, Abraham Kohn would discharge all the pastoral functions of the rabbi of the community at large, and
would especially supervise the new school to be established in
Lemberg in the near future, in both its religious and secular cur-
riculums.[4]

With this agreement in hand, Kohn returned to Hohenems,
but it took him longer to disengage himself from his duties there
than he had expected, and after visiting relatives in Vienna and
Bavaria, he and his family moved to Lemberg six months later
than agreed upon, arriving there in May, 1844, and settling in a
house on Benedictine Street that would, unbeknownst to him, be
his last earthly abode (and would later, after his murder, be renamed Kohn Street in his memory).

On 11 May 1844, Rabbi Abraham Kohn gave his first official
sermon as preacher in Lemberg, once more at the Great Synagogue. Given the importance of this occasion, attending the service were Archduke Ferdinand de Este, brother-in-law of the
emperor, the district military commander von Mülbacher, the
mayor Festenburg, and other civil and military officials, as well,
of course, the leaders of the Jewish community and the temple
committee.

Over fifty years later, Abraham Kohn's younger half-brother,
Bernhard, by then a typical upper-middle-class Viennese Jew
who looked down on the largely impoverished East European
Jews and especially their Yiddish language, described with much
malice the reaction of the traditional Lemberg Jews to his brother
Abraham's sermon:

> I was then a young boy of fifteen, and was bitterly depressed
> with the response to his first sermon. The new Temple, which he
> was to serve, was not yet built, and so the trial sermon was given
> at an Orthodox synagogue. The preacher had no illusions that he
> would have an audience in Lemberg as educated and intelligent
> as that in Hohenems, but he assumed at the very least that they
> would understand standard German, even though they spoke

Yiddish. But no one in Lemberg understood a word of what he said. I found myself among the audience, upset and angry at what they had heard: "*Was sugt er*" (What's he saying?) some asked, and others answered "*Datsch thut er schmüsen*! (He's speaking German)—and many there on that Saturday later tore their clothes in the sign of mourning, as at a funeral, since the synagogue was so defiled by standard German speech, instead of the clamor of the Jewish-Polish "jargon" they regarded as sacred."[5]

Clearly, this description cannot be taken as accurate, but it does reflect the deep cleavage between the masses of the Jewish community in Lemberg and the group that invited Abraham Kohn to preach there. Although a far greater proportion of the audience could probably understand Kohn's speech, or at least get its gist, than Berhard reported, they could hardly have been pleased by the fact that he was indeed speaking in German, as opposed to Yiddish, that he was wearing clerical garb reminiscent of Catholic clergy, and that, given the power of his supporters, there was a danger that he would one day be appointed Chief Rabbi of their city, the seat of so many great Eastern European rabbis over the centuries.

Nonetheless, immediately on his arrival, Rabbi Kohn began his functions with great enthusiasm, and while waiting for the new temple building to be completed, concentrated his efforts on establishing the new school for Jewish children in Lemberg, which he was able to open the next fall, enrolling 427 boys and girls for its first academic year. This number rose to 583 in 1845–1846, and to 738 in 1846–1847.[6]

The bare fact that in the heart of Galicia, so many Lemberg Jewish parents were willing to send so many of their children to a modernized, coeducational, Jewish school where the language of instruction was German and secular subjects were taught alongside Judaic studies, speaks volumes about the reality, as opposed to the mythology, of East European Jewry in the mid-nineteenth century. To be sure, we cannot assume that most of the students at this school, or their parents, were "modernist" or "progressive" (not to speak of "Reform") Jews in any meaningful sense of the terms: the motivation of most of these parents was undoubtedly quite simply to provide their children with an education that would enable them to succeed in the new economy and political reality that surrounded them. But attend the school they did, in droves, and to teach them appropriately, Rabbi Kohn introduced into the school the Hebrew grammar he had authored while in Hohenems, and wrote the two new textbooks already mentioned—a biblical history and a primer on Judaism for Jewish children.

Meanwhile, the construction of the Temple was proceeding apace, but it was occurring in a truly revolutionary political context that at first seemed to have little to do with the Jews or Rabbi Abraham Kohn but would soon be absolutely crucial to his life—and death. First and foremost, both 1845 and 1846 were terrible years economically in Galicia, primarily affecting the lives of the enserfed peasantry, who began even more than normally to resent their landlords' control over their lives. But the minds of a large number of these very same landlords, members of the Polish gentry and aristocracy, were not on their peasants' worries but on the struggle for Polish national freedom, whose leaders had been rebuilding their forces and their strategies since their great defeat in 1830–1831 by the Russians. Now, Polish nationalists in both the Prussian and the Austrian partitions joined those in the Russian-controlled lands to plot another large-scale insurrection. Their plan was to begin their rebellion in Galicia and Posen, and not in the Congress Kingdom or the Lithuanian lands, since the Austrian and Prussian armies had far fewer soldiers stationed in these territories than did the Russian tsar.[7] The date of the insurrection was set for 21–22 February 1846, but someone tipped off the Prussian authorities, who promptly arrested the ringleaders of the conspiracy.

The Austrian army then invaded the independent city of Cracow, but the predictions of the Polish patriots were accurate, and their forces easily defeated the Habsburg army. A "Polish National Government" was proclaimed, with its mission to spread liberation to all previous Polish lands, to emancipate the peasants, and to give equal rights to the Jews. But when Polish troops began to try to spread this platform beyond the borders of Cracow, they were shocked by the peasants' violent opposition to them: the serfs' hatred of their landlords was incalculably stronger than their commitment to Polish independence. The peasants, supported and encouraged by the Austrian authorities, began to kill the Polish army and landlords, and the *jacquerie* became even more intense as it spread eastward, where of course the peasants were mostly Ruthenians, and the destruction was enormous. But so it was even in Western Galicia: in the Tarnów district, for example, it was estimated that 90 percent of the noble manors were burned down, and two thousand landowners and their families killed.[8]

Finally, on 4 March 1846, Russian and Austrian troops attacked Cracow and quickly took control of the city. Other Austrian forces were sent to Lemberg and arrested conspirators found there. By November, Cracow had lost its independence and was annexed to Galicia, and the Polish national cause reeled under yet another calamitous failure.[9]

Although in retrospect, as one later historian was to put it, "for Galicia as a whole, the *jacquerie* of 1846 exposed the shortcomings of the existing authoritarian regime, [and] prepared the ground for eventual autonomy,"[10] at the time the Austrian regime regarded this defeat of the Poles as a great victory, and gloried in the support they received from the peasantry and from the Jews. The leaders of the Jewish community of Lemberg had, for example, volunteered to raise a Jewish brigade to support Austrian control of the city and of Galicia, but the authorities declined this request, claiming officially that the city and the province were safe, but that they were grateful for this display of patriotism, which they would take up should there be any need for it. (One can only imagine what they privately thought about the suitability of the Jews for such military action—an error that caught them by surprise two years later.) Instead, the Lemberg Jewish community contributed an enormous amount of liquor to the Austrian army, for which they received appropriate thanks.[11]

Assuming that their support of the Habsburg Empire would be repaid in kind, on 3 April 1846, the Lemberg Jewish communal officials submitted a petition to Emperor Ferdinand I, asking for the removal of Jewish residence restrictions in villages, claiming that allowing them to move outside the crowded cities would increase the "German element" and Austrian patriotism in the countryside. This petition was approved by the local authorities, but, like so many early requests, sat on the emperor's desk with no resolution.

Nonetheless, the Jews had in fact demonstrated their loyalty to the Austrian state, and this loyalty was appreciated by the authorities, and demonstrated quite overtly on Friday, 18 September 1846, when after six years of planning, the consecration of the new "progressive synagogue" of Lemberg was held. A squadron of Austrian cavalry in full military regalia lined the route leading from the Old Market Square to the doors of the temple, and at precisely 4 P.M., as the military commander of Galicia and his aides entered the temple, an army band struck up the national anthem of the Habsburg Empire.

The new temple was an impressive building, in the center of the city, topped with a dome visible from many parts of Lemberg. Under the lintel was proudly inscribed in Hebrew "*Beit yaakov lekhu ve-nelkha be'or adonai*" (House of Jacob, arise and go forth in the light of the Lord) (Isaiah 2:5), and above the entrance itself, a Hebrew inscription meaning "This is the gateway to the Lord." After the national anthem was played, the congregation was greeted by its president, Emanuel Blumenfeld, and then Rabbi Kohn took the stage and delivered a sermon based on Genesis 28:16: "Surely the Lord is in this place and I did not know it." This prooftext might seem a strange one for a consecration sermon—it might seem more appropriate for the opponents of the temple who did not recognize it as a House of God. But Kohn's point was, of course, the opposite: Jacob utters these words after he has left his father Isaac's home to seek a daughter of his mother's kin, and comes to a strange place he did not know before, where he falls asleep and dreams of a ladder stretching from heaven to earth, with angels of the Lord "ascending and descending" on it:

And behold, the Lord stood above it and said: "I am the Lord, God of Abraham your father and the God of Isaac; the land on which you lie I will give to you and to your descendants, and your descendants shall be like the dust of the earth . . . and by you and your descendants shall all families of the earth bless themselves. . . ." Then Jacob awoke from his sleep, and said: "Surely God is in this place and I did not know it."

The moral of the story was then made clear: the Jews had been exiled from their homeland for a millennium and a half, wandering about hopelessly and falling prey to the worst persecutions and calumnies, which caused them naturally to look askance at their neighbors, to turn inward, to indulge in superstitions and false beliefs based on fear, including mystical nonsense such as that which the Hasidic movement had recently fallen prey to, all the while forsaking the true religion that God had revealed to the Jewish people. Through these long centuries and travails they had, like Jacob their patriarch, been asleep, but now, as He did to Jacob in Bethel, God awoke them from their slumber, and showed them the way back to His Truth and His Torah. He inspired the gracious emperors of Austria to encourage the Jews to improve themselves, and permitted the local authorities to allow the Jews of Lemberg to build this *Bet-el*, this House of God, where He could be worshipped in the spirit of the true and living Judaism. This was a result not only of divine grace and imperial wisdom but also of the foresight of the leaders of the Jewish community of Lemberg who saw, in their own dreams, a ladder that could ascend from earth to heaven, a temple that would be a *sukkat shalom*, a tabernacle of peace, that, in line with God's promise to Jacob, would serve the Jews of Lemberg, of Galicia as a whole, and indeed would lead "all families of the earth [to] bless themselves" with the name of the Lord—"*Damit ale Völker der Erde erkennen, das der Ewige allein Gott ist, keiner sonst. Amen! Amen!* (Thereby, all the nations of the earth will know that the Eternal alone is God, and no one else, Amen, Amen!)—a sentiment that, although based on the traditional "Aleynu" prayer, clearly had Reform resonances in this context.[12]

So pleasing to the authorities was this sermon that soon thereafter they took a step that Emanuel Blumenfeld and Jacob Rappoport had barely dreamed about: after conferring with the local
authorities in Hohenems and with prominent and trustworthy
Austrian Jews such as Solomon Sulzer in Vienna, on 3 May 1847,
the government appointed Rabbi Kohn as *"Kreisrabbiner"* (District Rabbi) of Lemberg—in other words, the officially recognized Chief Rabbi of the Jewish community.[13]

This move, quite naturally, threw the Orthodox Jews of Lemberg and their leaders, both rabbinic and lay, into a frenzy, not
only because of what they perceived to be the insult to the memory of the great rabbis of Lemberg's past, but also, and for some
of them especially, since one of the District Rabbi's main responsibilities was to supervise the "metrical books" of the Jewish community, the official record of births, deaths, and the like, which
served, most important, as the basis on which the taxes of the
Jewish community were assessed. As noted, these included those
on kosher meat and on candles that were hated by the Jewish
masses and intelligentsia, but they also were a source of enormous income to those Orthodox Jews who farmed them out for
the government. In fact, previous to his appointment as District
Rabbi, the richest Jews of the community, the Orthodox Joseph
Hirsch Rappoport, Marcus Wolf Ettinger, Jakob Herz Bernstein,
and Hirsch Orenstein, had submitted a petition to the Austrian
authorities denouncing Rabbi Kohn as an unlearned Jew unfit to
serve as a rabbi in Lemberg, and demanding that the post of district rabbi be elected, as in the past, rather than appointed. But
this petition was rebuffed by the authorities, and thereupon
Bernstein and Orenstein began a campaign against Rabbi Abraham Kohn among the Orthodox masses of the city, both traditional and Hasidic. Rumors circulated that he desecrated the
Sabbath and ate nonkosher food; that the architectural model for
the Temple was the local Catholic cathedral; that when the temple was being built, the workmen would arrive each morning to
discover that—miraculously!—the bricks and mortar laid the
previous day had been torn down, and they would have to start
from scratch; that when Rabbi Kohn gave his first sermon in

town, he tore the curtain off the Holy Ark and stomped on it; that in response, the next morning the traditional Jews of Lemberg rent their clothing, symbolically sitting shivah for the death of Judaism in their city.

In fact, throughout his career as rabbi of the Lemberg Temple, the reforms we know Abraham Kohn to have introduced were those that he had already had instituted in Hohenems: decorum in the services, a cantor leading the prayers—which were all in Hebrew, save the prayer for the government, which was in German, as was of course the sermon; the abolition of the supplementary poems (*piyyutim*) on holidays, and the practice of selling the *aliyot* to the Torah; and the introduction of the confirmation ceremony, both for boys and for girls. Perhaps most radical, however, was his abolition of the requirement that married women cover their heads in the temple—a practice that is still commonly required today in many North American Conservative synagogues today. For this reason alone, the Lemberg Temple fully merits being called a "Reform temple" rather than simply a nontraditional synagogue.

Ironically, as his Orthodox opponents were plotting how best to oppose him and remove him from office and from the city, Abraham Kohn published a series of articles entitled *"Briefe aus Galizien"* (Letters from Galicia) in yet another German-Jewish periodical, Isidor Busch's *Kalendar und Jahrbuch für Israeliten* (Almanach and Yearbook for the Jews), published in Vienna, that contained a surprising assessment of Hasidism and its supporters in Galicia. Most Jewish enlighteners, especially in Galicia, had been denouncing this movement for decades, and most of Kohn's supporters in Lemberg undoubtedly believed that the Hasidim were the most obscurantist Jews of all, and their greatest enemy. Although, to be sure, Kohn decried the superstitions believed in by the masses of Hasidim, and their exploitation by their putative leaders, he sympathetically explained that their acceptance of this new form of popular Judaism was caused by the spiritual vacuum that had been created in Polish Jewry by the supremacy of a dry rabbinism that valued meaningless casuistry over religious faith, to the extent that marriages were based

on the extent of a potential groom's mastery of this pointless tal-
mudism. These points had already by 1846 oft been made in the
past, but Kohn moved on to a far more positive portrait of Hasidism that any of his predecessors among the maskilim or the
reformers:

> Although Hasidism is a return not only to childhood, but to
> childishness, in many ways it has far more worth, and certainly
> contains far more hope, than the worn-out and weary Talmudism
> that it replaced. It is, in its own way, a popular movement for re-
> form that can pave the way for a rational reform of the Jews. It
> certainly has brought more freedom into the synagogue, and per-
> mitted changes in the liturgy . . . that make the prayer-service, al-
> beit tasteless, still far more full of life and meaningful to its adher-
> ents than the dry bones it replaced.[14]

There is no indication that either the Hasidic or the other Orthodox Jews in Lemberg knew of these words, or for that matter,
his supporters. But soon, Rabbi Kohn became involved even
more publicly than before in an attempt to reform the legal status and taxes of the Jewish community of Lemberg and Galicia
as a whole. In the summer of 1847, Emanuel Blumenfeld called together the leaders of the Jewish communities of Lemberg, Brody,
Tarnopol, Stanisławów, Strij, and Sambor for a meeting to plan a
petition to the emperor protesting against the special Jewish
taxes as the cause of much devastation among the masses of
Galician Jewry, and asking, moreover, that the Jews in the cities
be granted full burgher rights alongside their Catholic neighbors.[15] A delegation was appointed, headed by Blumenfeld and
including District Rabbi Kohn, to travel to Vienna and to present
this petition to the emperor himself. This they did, but to little
effect: The requests about the Jewish taxes and town citizenship
were rejected, but one of their other requests was granted: the
prohibition of the traditional Jewish garb (as described above)—
a central point of Joseph II's reforms that had lain dormant for
more than half a century.

The Orthodox leaders understandably opposed this move,
and again gathered hundreds of signatures on a petition sent to

the authorities to allow them to retain their traditional dress, which—especially under the influence of Rabbi Moses Sofer of Pressburg, one of the leading rabbinic authorities of the age and the founder of what has come to be known as "ultra-Orthodoxy—they came to regard as not merely an external matter but also as a vital and immutable aspect of their religious identity.[16]

The governor of Galicia then formally asked District Rabbi Abraham Kohn for an opinion on this matter, and he answered in a lengthy ten-page memo, reviewing the history of the dress of East European Jewry and concluding, not surprisingly, that it was not a matter of authentic Jewish religious practice, and indeed presented a serious obstacle to the modernization of the Jews and their interaction with their Gentile neighbors. Moreover, in line with his previous writings (and rulings) on the subject, he particularly criticized the custom of women covering their hair, especially the widespread practice of doing so with elaborate head-coverings bedecked with jewels, which caused an economic burden on many Jewish families, led to unhealthy material competition among Jewish women themselves, and evoked the hostility and envy of their Gentile neighbors, who imagined, incorrectly, that the Jews were therefore all rich, when in fact they more than often were not. He therefore recommended that the traditional garb be permitted only for rabbis and other clerics, and that the granting of the right to marriage, as well as any commercial privileges, be based upon the adoption of modern, German-style, dress among the Jews. Though this recommendation, coming from another Jew, was undoubtedly shocking to contemporary traditional Jews, it was in fact in line with similar recommendations submitted by Jewish enlighteners from the late eighteenth century on, both in Galicia and in the Russian Empire.[17]

At the same time, the authorities asked the opinion of this matter of the secretary of the Lemberg Jewish community, Meir Mintz, who—as mentioned earlier—though an "enlightener" was sympathetic to the Orthodox community and especially antipathetic to Rabbi Kohn. Mintz's memo, later published as a separate brochure, argued that the obstacle to the Jews' cultural progress was not their dress but their political status, and that the only solution to their plight was their immediate emancipation.[18]

Mintz's response to the authorities was submitted at roughly the same time as yet another petition was sent to the authorities by his Orthodox colleagues, upping the ante against the leadership of the Lemberg community and their rabbi, by claiming that with their knowledge and approval, the police inspector of the Jewish community, Hirsch Zipper, was taking bribes from Jews outside Lemberg to support the temple.[19] All of these petitions and cross-petitions, accusations and counteraccusations, left the Galician authorities, and their Viennese superiors, mightily confused about how to handle the fractious Jewish community of the Galician capital.

But all too soon, these questions receded into the background for two reasons that seemed unrelated, but would soon intersect: In January 1848, while walking home from work one day, Rabbi Abraham Kohn was set on by a gang of Orthodox Jews and beaten up. The Jewish police officials in Lemberg were called to investigate this attack, but no action was taken, at Rabbi Kohn's request.

And then, a few weeks later, revolution broke out in Paris, Berlin, and Vienna as well as the other major centers of Western and Central Europe, and soon, spread to Lemberg as well, with repercussions no one could possibly have predicted.

Revolution and Murder

O<small>N</small> 24 FEBRUARY 1848, KING Louis Philippe of France abdicated his throne, succumbing to the demands of the workers and students of Paris who had seized control of the capital, demanding revolutionary change. That evening the Second Republic was proclaimed, and the struggle between the so-called rightwing and leftwing revolutionary forces began, arguing over the future of a new, free, France. Inspired by these events, in mid-March, popular demonstrations broke out in Berlin, barricades were set up in the streets, and King Frederick William, hoping to avoid the fate of Louis Phillippe, almost immediately began to make concessions to quell the fury: he abolished censorship, promised a new, liberal, constitution, and even paraded through the streets of Berlin wearing the tricolor of black, red, and gold, recently adopted as the flag of the new, revolutionary Germany. In Vienna, barricades were set up in the streets by students and workers, mass demonstrations followed, and soon, the revolution spread to Budapest, where Louis Kossuth denounced the imperial regime and demanded responsible government for Hungary.

The Habsburg Emperor Ferdinand I responded to these events in panic, firing the all-but-universally hated Metternich, who fled the country. On 15 March 1848, Ferdinand abolished censorship, promised the convocation of a constituent assembly, and, most shockingly of all, immediately accepted the demands of the Hungarians for negotiations regarding autonomy within the Habsburg Empire. Within days, the revolution spread to the provincial capitals—including Milan, Prague, Brünn, and Lemberg as well.

Here, on 18 March 1848, for the first time in their history, masses of Poles, Ruthenians, and Jews demonstrated arm-in-arm in front of the governor's mansion and proclaimed solidarity against the Austrian autocracy. Local Polish nationalist leaders who had served time in Austrian prisons drew up a petition demanding autonomy for Galicia with anative administration headed by a parliament representing all classes and ethnic groups, a National Guard, Polish as the language of instruction in the schools, amnesty for all political prisoners, the abolition of serfdom, and equal rights for all citizens, regardless of religion. The next day—Purim, according to the Jewish calendar, the joyous carnival festival celebrating the liberation of the Jews from a murderous enemy—Jewish leaders advised their community to sign this petition, which included a demand (authored by none other than Rabbi Abraham Kohn) for the Jews' longed-for emancipation and the abolition of the taxes specific to them. Thousands of Jews acceded to this advice, and that afternoon, joined a massive demonstration, some twenty thousand strong, to present the petition to the governor. The Ruthenian Count Sapieha, the Polish nationalist Florian Ziemiałkowski, the head of the Jewish community Rahmiel Mieses, and Rabbi Abraham Kohn marched at the head of the demonstration.

Meanwhile, even more radical revolutionaries arrived in town from Cracow and convinced the local leadership to help form a delegation representing all of Galicia to present their demands directly to the emperor in Vienna. This delegation included Rabbi Kohn and his colleague from Cracow, Rabbi Dov-Berish Meisels, famous among Poles and Jews alike for his Polish nationalism and help to the Polish cause in the 1846 uprising. The delegation arrived in Vienna on 31 March; only a small part of it, including Rabbi Meisels, was selected to meet with the emperor in person, which they did on 6 April. Ferdinand agreed to take the petition seriously, even though it demanded the reversal of the partition of Poland, and called the accession of Galicia by Austria "illegal." Giving up Galicia would clearly lead to war with Russia, as was made exceptionally clear by St. Petersburg, which would under no circumstances tolerate a return to the borders of 1772.

Count Franz Stadion, the governor of Galicia,[1] was essentially on his own in the face of the mass movement in the streets of Lemberg, since the imperial regime in Vienna was hardly in any shape to transmit instructions to the provinces. He therefore acted both boldly and prudently: on the one hand, he abolished censorship in Galicia, released political prisoners, and agreed to the formation of a National Guard—essentially a Galician army, which was largely Polish, although it included a significant number of Jews, who formed a separate brigade that numbered approximately three hundred men in Lemberg.[2] On the other hand, he secretly sent a missive to the governors of the other Austrian provinces, warning against the potential danger to the empire and did not accede to the Lemberg crowd's demands either for an immediate granting of autonomy to Galicia, or, most important, for the abolition of serfdom. Also in secret, he sent a message to leading Ruthenians warning them about their potential treatment under a Polish autonomous regime. The old stategy of divide and conquer had, after all, proved so successful but two years earlier.

In mid-April, he again tried to kill two birds with one stone. To secure the support of both the Ruthenian peasantry and the Polish and Jewish revolutionaries, while plotting ultimately to set them against one another, he announced the abolition of serfdom in Galicia. Thus, the Galician peasants were liberated from their landlords several months ahead of their counterparts in the rest of the Austrian Empire.[3] As we shall see, even after all the other accomplishments of the Revolution of 1848 were reversed, including the emancipation of the Jews, this central event in East European history remained in effect, and the economic and social status of the now liberated peasantry and their previous owners had to be renegotiated.

For the Jews, the most complex issue that the revolution brought on was that of solidarity with Polish nationalist aspirations versus loyalty to the Austrian state. The vast majority of the Jews adhered to the traditional principle of loyalty to whatever regime was in power. This strategy had sustained the Jews throughout their history in the Diaspora, and the rabbis long had interpreted such loyalty as following the divine will. Thus, one can assume that most traditional Jews remained loyal to the Habsburg throne throughout the events of the spring and summer of 1848, though they were hardly enthusiastic about the restrictions on their lives and the taxes imposed on them by the regime. It was the modernizing Jews of Galicia, by contrast, who were in a quandary: since 1772, they had steered a careful course, adhering to a firm policy of fidelity to the Josephinian legacy of Germanization and self-improvement of the Jews, as the surest road both to political and to religious and cultural liberation—at the same time as the government itself had essentially abandoned the hallmarks of Joseph's Enlightenment-based policies. Thus, without overtly displaying any disloyalty to the regime, they argued continually against the restrictions on Jewish residence rights (even Emanuel Blumenfeld had problems getting permission for his second wife to move to Lemberg before he could marry her!), and of course, against the candle and kosher-meat taxes. But already in the 1830s, after the collapse of the Polish Uprising of 1831 and its brutal suppression by the Russian army, some Galician Jews—including most famously, Rabbi Meisels and much less well known, the Lemberg maskil Meir Mintz—became sympathetic to the Polish national cause, especially due to the recognition that as a result of the German proclivities of the Jewish elite, anti-Jewish sentiment was rising among the Polish nationalists, especially the nobility. However, as we have seen, the Jews en masse demonstrated anew their loyalty to the Austrian state during the 1846 Polish rebellion.

But rather quickly in 1848 it became clear to the leaders of the Galician Jewish enlighteners and bourgeoisie that they had to make an abrupt change in their basic orientation: the rebellion against the authoritarianism of the Austrian regime in favor of a liberal polity that would grant equal rights to all residents—or now "citizens" in the new meaning of the term—of Galicia, was intimately and inextricably linked to the ultimate victory of Polish demands for autonomy. Jewish emancipation was at stake, and thus they made a 180-degree volte-face in regard to the Polish national movement. Typical of their reaction was an oft-quoted poem by the local *maskil* Maurycy Rappoport, entitled "*Gruss an die Freiheit"* (Salute to Freedom), which expressed sympathy, in German of course, with the Polish freedom fighters who fell in the battle against the Austrian regime:

> The chains have fallen off, which bound
> So many heroes,
> And decked with ornaments of freedom,
> We greet our brothers! (*Begrüssen wir die Brüder!"*[4]

For his part, Abraham Kohn was between a rock and a hard place: as a Bohemian-born and educated German-speaking reformist rabbi, he had believed for decades that the spread of the German language and German culture, along with modern Jewish theology and scientifically updated practices, was the surest combination for Jewish liberation. As a political liberal, he abhorred the authoritarianism of the Vienna regime, but his preferred solution was clearly a liberalization of that regime rather than the dissolution of the Austrian Empire into ethnic ministates. By contrast, he was a convinced democrat, and democracy for Galicia meant majority rule—in other words, that of the Poles, although with the guarantee of political equality and religious freedom for the almost equally numerous Ruthenians, and of course, for the Jews as well. He had, in fact, himself drafted Point 9 of the petition to the regime, which called for religious freedom and the abolition of taxes specific to religious denominations. Moreover, he was supremely conscious of the fact that he was a foreigner in Lemberg and that he had to accede to the political realities of his adopted community and its best interests. Indeed, even though his support for the Polish cause in the course of the Revolution was doubted by some of the leaders of the Polish nationalist movement—Ziemiałkowski in particular, did not trust him[5]—by May 1848 he had come fully to embrace the Polish national program for Galicia, and drafted a statement to the Poles and Ruthenians under the banner of "Liberty, Equality, and Fraternity" urging them to work together with the Jews to obtain freedom for all.[6]

In the midst of all this political turmoil and excitement, however, Kohn's personal safety and his professional security were threatened by his Orthodox opponents in Lemberg, led again, by the tax-farmers who feared that the revolutionary stirrings might lead to the abolition of the taxes that made them so extraordinarily wealthy. A new petition was sent to the local and the imperial authorities denouncing Rabbi Kohn as the source of all the problems afflicting the Jews of Lemberg, and on 23 April 1848, during the Passover holiday, a crowd of Orthodox Jews descended on the Jewish communal offices, demanding his removal from the district rabbinate. Fearing that this would lead to violence, the secretary of the Jewish community, Bernhard Piepes, had the leader of this crowd, Joel Schorr, arrested, but to no avail: the mob moved on to the building in which Rabbi Kohn lived on Benedictine Street, and began to throw rocks at the windows of his flat, with glass shattering everywhere. Only the arrival of the National Guard, with both Jewish and Polish armed officers, broke up the crowd and prevented bodily harm to Rabbi Kohn and his family. Several more Orthodox Jews were arrested, but Rabbi Kohn refused to press charges against them, and they were released.[7]

One of the unanswered—and still basically unanswerable—questions hovering over this entire matter and its later ramifications is why the Orthodox majority of Lemberg Jews did not oppose the taxes and resent the wealth of the tax-farmers, garnered out of their pockets? We can only speculate that as in many other circumstances in the past and present, "the masses" do not always—or even usually—act in their own self-interest, especially when such self-interest conflicts with traditional religious and social structures that are not only familiar, but ratified, and at times even sanctified, by their religious and political leaders. Clearly, in this case, the fact that the leader of the movement to abolish these taxes was a Reform rabbi dedicating to transforming the Judaism they knew and time-honored customs in traditional Jewish life that they believed to be immutable, served only to reinforce the "masses'" allegiance to their leaders, however much that conflicted with their economic self-interest.

Given the refusal of the Jewish community to transmit the petitions of the Orthodox opponents of Rabbi Kohn to the authorities, these petitions were secretly published as two

German-language brochures widely circulated throughout the city: *An Open Letter from the Petitioners and so-called Supporters of Orthodox Judaism against District Rabbi Abraham Kohn in Lemberg*[8] and *Some Words from the Signators of the Petition Regarding District Rabbi Abraham Kohn.*[9] In essence, both pamphlets complained that given the hold of the "progressive" minority of the Jews of Lemberg on the communal leadership, the vast majority could not have its views expressed freely in public; despite the fact that they had collected thousands of signatures supporting their petition, they were prevented by the Jewish plutocrats from presenting these views to the authorities. Most centrally, they charged that Abraham Kohn was totally unfit to be a rabbi in Lemberg, not to speak of the District Rabbi: he was totally ignorant of the Talmud and its laws, and was therefore unable to resolve religious disputes among the Jews of Lemberg on the basis of rabbinic law, or to approve rabbis to serve in local positions throughout the Lemberg district, as his position required. Moreover, he was personally irreligious, broke major commandments of Judaism, and as a result had become not only an embarrassment but also a laughing-stock, among the vast majority of the Jews of the city, who therefore demanded his immediate dismissal. This demand was not based, the authors stressed, on an opposition to modern education on the part of Orthodox Jews: They realized that the new times required new educational strategies to teach their children how to live in contemporary society. But Rabbi Kohn's extreme views on these matters were only supported by a couple of hundred of his supporters in Lemberg, who thus distorted the democratic will of the Jewish community in the Galician capital. Finally, the Orthodox authors cynically played their final card: although they supported the Habsburg ancien regime and not the Polish nationalists, they emphasized that they wanted a *Polish* rabbi, not a foreign one.[10] To be sure, not a word was mentioned in these petitions and brochures about the huge profits that accrued to the leaders of the Orthodox opposition from the candle and kosher slaughtering taxes, and Rabbi Kohn's strident opposition to these taxes.

Realizing the gravity of the situation, a meeting was called between Rabbi Kohn's opponents and his supporters to try to resolve the mounting tensions over him, but the leaders of the opposition, the Orthodox tax-farmers Bernstein and Orenstein
refused to back down from their demands that Kohn leave Lemberg at once, and offered only to buy out his contract for a substantial sum. Fearful for her husband and family, Magdalena
Kohn pleaded with her husband to accept this offer, but he refused, believing, as he was reported to have said, "I am after all,
among Jews, what will they do to me in the end?"[11]

In any event, the authorities disregarded these pamphlets,
brochures, and petitions, and Governor Stadion soon named
Rabbi Kohn to join the clerical advisory board summoned to
provide him counsel in regard to the National Assembly for
Galicia demanded by the rebels. Unbeknownst to Rabbi Kohn,
this was actually an attempt by Stadion to subvert the Revolution by coopting the clerical leadership of the Polish, Ruthenian,
and Jewish communities. In the event this advisory board met
with Stadion several times but its work came to naught, especially as in June Stadion was called to Vienna to serve as Minister of Internal Affairs of the empire as a whole.

In the imperial capital, he brought the demands of the progressive Galician Jews regarding their taxes to the Ministry of Finance,
with the recommendation that they be abolished forthwith. The
government as a whole agreed, but accepted the amendment pro-
posed by the Treasury Minister that the immediate abolition of
these taxes would cost the central government the huge sum of
80,000 Florins, and so delayed the implementation of the decision
until the end of 1848.[12]

In fact, even by the time this decision was made, signs of the
fading out of the Revolution were becoming clear. In France, the
farcical replay of the first French Revolution was beginning,
as the fragile coalition of moderates and radicals began to fall
apart, leading to mounting violence and bloodshed. On 15 May,
a workers' protest took over the National Assembly and set up a
provisional government, but the weakness of this government
encouraged the supporters of reaction to recoup, leading to the

infamous June Days Uprising, in which the forces loyal to the ancien regime killed over fourteen hundred people in the streets of Paris. A "temporary dictator" was put in charge of the country, and he promptly reinstated censorship and suppressed the dissidents. By the end of the year, Prince Louis Napoleon became president of the republic, surrounded himself with monarchists, and the National Assembly became essentially obsolete; the Second Republic would soon turn into the Second Empire. In Germany, where the goal of the revolution was the unification of all German-speaking territories under a liberal regime, territorial conflicts—especially the fight with Denmark over Schleswig-Holstein—began to defang the revolutionary forces. By the autumn of 1848, the Right had gained control in the parliament, leading to the reassertion of royal authority by King Frederick William, and by the end of the year, to the dissolution of the Prussian constituent assembly and the establishment of a new parliamentary system which gave power back to the monarchy and nobility. In Austria, already on 26 April government troops attacked Cracow and retook control of the city, and on 11 June they bombarded Prague during the convening there of a Slav Congress. A day earlier, the new parliament promised by the emperor, the *Reichstag*, was convened, with representation from all segments of the population, including the peasantry and the Jews. Slowly, Stadion's strategy began to prove itself correct once again: after the emancipation of the serfs of the entire empire was promulgated on 22 July, the peasant representatives—and especially the Galician Ruthenians—lost their incentive to rebel, and quickly proved more loyal to the Austrian authorities than to the Polish nationalist leaders. On 24 July, the Austrian army retook Lombardy, regaining control of the crucial Italian territories of the empire, and on 17 September began an invasion of Hungary. These military triumphs soon rebounded to Vienna itself, and on 31 October the capital was bombarded back into submission and the radical leaders were executed. Lemberg was the next target, and in November it was attacked and retaken by the imperial army, and Galicia as a whole was restored to firm Habsburg control. On 2 December,

King Ferdinand was forced to abdicate the throne by forces looking for a stronger monarch not bound by any promises of reform, and his son Franz-Joseph became emperor.

Undoubtedly emboldened by this pan-European and local
turn of events, the wealthy Orthodox opponents of Rabbi Abraham Kohn stepped up their attack against him. In August 1848,
Kohn wrote to his brother Bernhard in Vienna that the stirrings
of the mob against him were increasing, that the Jewish communal council was essentially destroyed and could not control the
situation, and that he feared for the future.[13] In early September
placards were attached to the walls of the Orthodox synagogues
of the city attacking the Reform rabbi in the strongest terms yet:
he was a *poshea yisrael*—a renegade, sinful Jew, who had to be
unseated from his post as district rabbi at all costs. Probably
fearing even more violence in the streets, on Saturday, 2 September, Rabbi Kohn preached a sermon in the Lemberg Temple on
the theme of "Thou Shalt Not Kill," emphasizing both the biblical and the rabbinic animus to violence. But four days later, at
mid-day on 6 September 1848, an Orthodox Jew entered the
kitchen of the Kohn household, and pretended to light his cigar
over the flame of the stove. As he bent over to do so, he stealthily poured a vial of arsenic into the soup pot boiling on the
stove. That evening, the family sat down to dinner, began to eat
the soup, and soon all fell sick. Doctors were summoned, including Jacob Rappoport, but they could only save Magdalena Kohn
and the four older children. The Kohn's infant daughter Teresa,
and the forty-one-year-old Rabbi Abraham Kohn, died the next
day of arsenic poisoning.

That afternoon, the local Polish newspaper, the *Gazeta Narodowa,*
published the following report:

> Yesterday at mid-day a horrible crime took place in Lemberg.
> The entire family of the local rabbi was poisoned. For a long time,
> the Orthodox Jews had been waging a continuing battle against
> the Reform Jews. The regime gave the entire community a rabbi
> supported by the Reformers, which the Orthodox never stopped
> protesting against. These sects are as different from one another

as can be, and the Orthodox therefore demanded an Orthodox rabbi. Right from the start of the constitutional era, they began to attack Rabbi Kohn, storming his house, beating him up on the street. Now, to rid themselves of him, they upped the ante to a crime, obviously the result of a previously planned conspiracy: an Orthodox Jew stealthily came into the kitchen, to use the fire, and took the opportunity to drop a portion of arsenic unnoticed in the soup pot. The entire family and the servants—totaling nine persons—got sick on the spot. Doctors immediately appeared at the scene. Up to now, the rabbi and one of his children have died, and the others are but clinging to life, but it is not clear if they can be saved.

Several Jews have been arrested, are being held for investigation. Last night, the ailing maid could not recognize the guilty party from among this group.[14]

Meanwhile, on the next day, Abraham Kohn's funeral was attended by "[r]epresentatives of the state and the district authorities, the *kahal*, the synagogue board, and thousands of people . . . but not a single Orthodox Jew in a long coat was to be seen."[15] At the temple, he was eulogized by the man who brought him to Lemberg, Emanuel Blumenfeld,[16] and his body was then brought to the Jewish cemetery and buried in its most honored section reserved for the town's rabbis, and right next to the late chief rabbi, Rabbi Jacob Orenstein. At the cemetery, two of the teachers at the school established by Rabbi Kohn spoke about their mentor, mourning him as a martyr in Israel. One stressed the horror that this deed had been done by a fellow Jew, motivated by the "wild cannibal lust of a poisoner in a Jewish caftan," whereas the other cited the noted rabbinic dictum, "So long as a righteous man lives in a city, he is its glory, its honor, its luster. When he leaves, that glory, that honor, and that luster, depart as well." It is unclear whether the eulogist was aware of a tragic irony: this dictum was cited by the most famous Jewish exegete of all time, Rashi, in his comments on the biblical portion that includes Jacob's dream of the ladder stretching from heaven to earth, which had served, as we saw, as the prooftext for Rabbi Kohn's first sermon at the Lemberg Temple. The dream of a "sukkat shalom"—a tabernacle of peace—that Abraham Kohn had wished for in that first sermon less than two years earlier, had been twisted into a tabernacle of death.[17]

And even the site of his burial became an object of threatened controversy and perhaps even real-life desecration, since some of the Orthodox and especially Hasidic Jews of Lemberg were shocked at the fact that Abraham Kohn was buried among the late great Orthodox rabbis and scholars of Lemberg, and threatened to remove the corpse from its grave. For several days, Jewish members of the National Guard stood watch over Rabbi Kohn's tomb to protect it from zealous marauders. Nonetheless, rumors spread throughout Lemberg that his body was in fact later exhumed, and thrown into an anonymous pit at the cemetery— although his tombstone remained in place among the great rabbis of Lemberg's past.[18]

Four days later, a second article appeared in the newspaper with more details:

> The main instigator of the poisoning of the rabbi's family has been revealed. He is the goldsmith Pilpel. At first, he hid himself: it seems that he fled from the city, but on the day of the rabbi's funeral he appeared in a barbershop to have his beard shaven off and his long hair cut. This brought him to the attention of several youths who were present, who reported this to the local Guardsmen, who quickly took him into custody. He was also identified by the seven-year-old daughter of the rabbi, even though she had been shown several other possible culprits. This was further confirmed by the maid who served in the house and was present at the crime. Before he came into the kitchen, he entered into several other kitchens in the same building and asked which one was the rabbi's.[19]

IT IS AT THIS POINT that both misinformation and ideologically based distortions of the assassination of Rabbi Abraham Kohn begin. Some accounts merely get the facts wrong: the date of the murder is mistated;[20] a son of the Kohn family instead of a daughter is said to have died[21] or Teresa is said to have died a day after her father.[22] Even the most reliable historian of Lemberg Jewry, N. M. Gelber, incorrectly states that Ber Pilpel "was sentenced in the first instance with the death penalty."[23] But several other authors clearly aim at covering up the role of Orthodox Jews in the assassination: as cited earlier, probably the most frequently consulted source about Jewish Lemberg or Abraham Kohn, the *Encyclopedia Judaica*, deliberately and rather shockingly obfuscates the matter, writing "After Kohn and his son [*sic*!] died from food poisoning [*sic*!] murder was suspected. An investigation was ordered by the authorities, and the leaders of the Orthodox sector, [Jacob Naphtali Herz] Bernstein and Hirsch Orenstein, were arrested. After a time, both were released for lack of evidence."[24] Another Orthodox author repeats this half-truth in his history of Lemberg Jewry in a major series of memorial books to important Jewish communities published after the Holocaust by one of the most important Orthodox institutions in Israel, *Mosad Harav Kook*,[25] and in another major memorial book to Lemberg Jewry, sums up the event with the statement that Rabbi Kohn died of criminal poisoning and leaves it at that—contrary to the evidence that was at his disposal at the time.[26] On the other side of the ideological divide, several secular scholars write with certainty that "the Orthodox gang" led by Bernstein and Orenstein hired a "noted murderer" to kill Rabbi Kohn.[27] One anti-Orthodox writer was certain that a formal *Sanhedrin*—a supreme rabbinical court—had authorized the killing of Abraham Kohn, basing itself on Maimonides's laws concering the treatment of heretics; and a later Zionist activist, writing in the immediate aftermath of the murder of the Labor Zionist leader Haim Arlosoroff in 1933, was convinced that Bernstein and Orenstein would not have ordered this murder without halachic justification, and debated which traditional legal source they relied on.[28]

The most neutral and reliable authors, basing themselves largely on the reports in the *Gazeta Narodowa* and in the German-Jewish press, as well as on a letter written by Magdalena Kohn to her brother-in-law Bernhard Kohn several months after the

PART **TWO**

The Investigation, Sentence, and Appeal

Abraham Ber Pilpel, Murderer?

I{.N THE STATE} archives of the city of L'viv, a file was recently located that had been catalogued but kept from the public's eye during the Soviet rule over the city from September 1939 to August 1991: File No. 150, Division 2, Subject 16, Item 2 of the Central State Archive of the Ukrainian Soviet Socialist Republic in the city of L'vov, Department of the Supreme District Court of L'vov, Appellate Division, entitled "Case of the Accused in the Murder of Abraham Kohn," opened in 1848 and closed in 1851. Although the cover page of this file says it consists of 100 pages, in fact, there are 202 pages in this thick packet, and this is only part of the materials relating to Rabbi Kohn in the L'viv archive.[1] All of these materials were written in many different hands in the Gothic German script of the nineteenth century, which even highly educated native German speakers today cannot make heads or tails of.[2]

Moreover, given the nature of the material—court decisions of three levels of the nineteenth-century Austrian judicial system (the Lemberg Criminal Court, the Galician District Appellate Court, and the Imperial Supreme and Cassation Court)—there is a great deal of duplication and repetition in these files.[3] To make sense of this extremely complicated newly discovered material, I will deal first with the case of the man charged with the actual murder of Rabbi Kohn, Abraham Ber Pilpel, and follow the police and court proceedings in his regard, which differ substantially from the standard account summarized in the previous chapter. I will then move on, in the next chapters, to the other Orthodox Jews charged with conspiring with Pilpel to commit the murder;

and finally follow the lengthy—and rather surprising—appeals process engaged in by Magdalena Kohn, which is not mentioned at all in any of the extant literature on her husband.

The file on Abraham Ber Pilpel begins with a general account of the murder of Rabbi Kohn, from the point of view of the Lemberg Criminal Court.

On 6 September 1848, District Rabbi Abraham Kohn, his wife, and four children (the fifth was with her wet-nurse) sat down to eat their usual mid-day meal. As soon as Mrs. Kohn served the soup to her family and tasted the first spoonful, she felt a burning sensation in her mouth, as if she had just gulped down some hard liquor. Her husband complained about the soup, too, but she thought that the cook had simply put too much pepper in it, and then proceeded, along with her son Gotthilf, to eat a bowlful of it. When the children began to feel ill, she went to the kitchen to ask the cook what vegetables or herbs she had put into the soup to make it green. She found the cook sick as well, having eaten the meat from the soup but not the liquid itself. Alarmed—and immediately fearing poisoning—Mrs. Kohn summoned the nearest physician, a Doctor Hensel, who at once administered emetics to everyone, and sent a sample of the soup for chemical testing to the pharmacy of Gabriel Mülling. Meanwhile, the whole Kohn family and their cook were bedridden, looking pale and strained, and Rabbi Kohn was so ill that he couldn't even respond to questioning. More doctors and surgeons arrived to treat the patients. The rest of the soup and meat was seized by the police as evidence (*corpus delicti*) and, in their presence, was formally determined by the local Professor Dr. Gloisner and the pharmacist Mülling to be laced with arsenic. As soon as poisoning was confirmed, at 5 P.M. that afternoon, a criminal investigation was begun.

Rabbi Kohn died at 3 A.M. the next morning, the 7th of September 1848, and thereafter, the contents of his stomach and duodenum were examined and found to contain traces of arsenic, leading to the official conclusion by the city pathologists that his death "occurred as a result of poisoning of the entire organism, and hence was caused by artificial rather than natural means."[4] The same conclusion was reached regarding the Kohn's infant daugher Teresa, who died later that day—clearly (although not stated in the documents) she had been fed some of the soup, either by the wetnurse or by someone else.

This poisoning was therefore determined to be an assassination, according to the Austrian Imperial Criminal Code articles 117 and 118, which listed "assassination by poisoning" as the first category of murder as defined under Austrian law.[5] Moreover, the Lemberg authorities immediately speculated that Rabbi Kohn's assassination was the result of the bitter struggle against him on the part of a segment of the Orthodox Jews of the city. These Jews had most recently petitioned the government in August 1848 demanding that he be removed from the office of District Rabbi, but this demand was rejected, as Rabbi Kohn enjoyed the confidence of the authorities, including that of former governor, and now Minister of the Interior, Stadion.[6] Indeed, this Orthodox opposition, led by the richest Jews in the city, had begun to submit similar petitions, signed with hundreds of names, even before Rabbi Kohn originally arrived in Lemberg, arguing that he was irreligious, that he would cost the community as a whole too much, and that the Jews had always had the right to elect their rabbi, not have one imposed on them by the authorities.[7] The strife was intensified by his appointment on 3 May 1847 as District Rabbi of Lemberg, a position that gave him authority over the "metrical books" of the community, as well as by several sermons that Rabbi Kohn preached in the temple about the abolition of various traditional Jewish customs and in favor of a "reconciliation" between Jews and Christians.[8] The Orthodox then added to their accusations of his irreligiosity and ignorance of the Talmud and Jewish law a new charge, found to be without any basis: that he had tampered illegally with the records of the Jewish community.

After the promulgation of the new constitution in 1848 on 28 April and 5 May the Orthodox party again submitted petitions to remove Rabbi Kohn from his office, and these were answered by counterpetitions from the progressive Jews, leading to an official investigation of the matter by the Galician authorities, which once more concluded, on 6 August 1848, that there was no cause to remove Rabbi Kohn from his position.[9] Before and after this date, Rabbi Kohn had suffered numerous personal insults and threats on the part of Orthodox Jews.

On this basis, immediately after determining officially that poisoning had occurred, on the afternoon of 6 September, the criminal investigators stated that there was an "extreme likelihood that the poisoning of Abraham Kohn resulted from religious fanaticism. Therefore, on that day, thirty-six known enemies of the victim and members of the Orthodox community were imprisoned, including Herz Bernstein, Hirsch Orenstein, Abraham Weinreb, Isaac Schramek, Gabriel Suchestoff, and Matis Urech."[10]

Although there was a long-standing practice in European history to round up the leaders of Jewish—and other "minority"— communities when a crime was committed by one of their members, this was not the usual practice on the part of Habsburg authorities in the nineteenth century in regard to crimes committed by Jews, and must be explained by the specific circumstances of this case.

At the Kohns' residence, suspicion first fell on one Chaja Karpel, the daughter of the tavern-keeper Chaim Karpel who lived in the same building as the Kohns and was known as a bitter enemy of the rabbi. Chaja had come into the Kohns' kitchen on that morning to warm her coffee on the stove, and hence had access to the soup pot. But this suspicion was put aside when Mindel Fischler, the Kohns' cook, reported that she had kept her eyes on Chaja the entire time she was in the kitchen, and could see that she did no wrong.

Then, the Kohns' son Jacob reported to the police that he had been pursued by Orthodox youths threatening him that they all had arsenic in their possession, and that his father was going to die.[11]

The police then took the following testimonies about the events of that day:

Mindel Fischler, the Kohns' cook, eighteen years old, testified under oath that on the morning of 6 September, she lit the fire to begin to prepare the family's mid-day meal of beef, and that around noon, when she was peeling potatoes along with the Kohns' eight-year-old daughter Angelica, a Jew unknown to her appeared in the kitchen: he was tall, around thirty years old, with a gaunt face and a black beard covering his lips and chin, a long, hooked nose thin on top and broad on the bottom, and dressed in traditional Jewish garb (*jüdisch gekleideit*), with a long black coat and a tall black hat. He did not say a word to anyone, approached the stove where the meal was cooking and bent over it. His hat slipped off his head and he set it straight, at which point Mindel noticed that his other hand was shaking over the fire, and she thought he was trying to light the cigar that he had in his mouth. Given their respective positions, she could only see him from the side.

Angelica Kohn testified to the same effect, although as a child she was not put under oath. She added that at the time of the event she wasn't certain about what she had seen, but after the poisoning was revealed, it dawned on her that the man had taken something out of his pocket and put it into the soup pot while he was leaning over it. Her description of the suspect matched that of Mindel Fischer.[12]

The next witness was Freyde Werthheimer, the eighteen-year-old servant of Leib Necheles, a businessman who lived on the same floor of the Kohns' building. She testified that at around noon of the day in question, the suspect—whom she described in the same terms as the other witnesses—appeared in her kitchen, asking to light his cigar on the stove, and then asked if this was the kitchen of the Kohn family. She told him it was not, and pointed him to the other side of the staircase. He responded that he thought it wasn't the rabbi's kitchen or stove, since he saw that the meat was being salted according to the laws of kashrut, which he was sure did not happen in the rabbi's kitchen; and then he left.

Had the witnesses in this case been solely maids, cooks, and one child, it is less likely that the story they told would have been credible to the authorities—or later, to us. But they were not alone in telling this story. Another tenant in the building was Chaim Waitz, the agent of the local businessman Brühl. His seventeen-year-old servant, Riva (who did not have a surname) testified under oath that at around 11:45 A.M. on the morning of the 6th, a Jew—whom she described in the same manner as the others—came into the front part of her apartment, where the kitchen was located, and asked if he could light his cigar. She was busy cleaning the apartment and didn't respond, and he asked two more times, whereupon she said he didn't have to repeat himself so often, and could light the cigar that was in his mouth. At this point, her boss Esther Waitz and the wet-nurse Elisabeth Szostakowa were with her and saw the man, but did not speak with him.

Her description was confirmed by her mistress Esther Waitz, who testified under oath that a few minutes before noon, as she was standing in the kitchen dealing with her child, along with her wet-nurse Elisabeth Szostokowa and cook Riva, a Jew unknown to her entered her kitchen, with a short cigar in his mouth, and asked the cook if he could light that cigar; the cook did not answer him at first, but then gave him permission to light his cigar, at which point he laughed and said that his cigar was already lit, and then left the room. She did not have the opportunity to see him very clearly, but her description jibed with those of the previous witnesses. Elizabeth Szostokowa, the Waitz's twenty-two-year-old wet-nurse, confirmed these details under oath as well.

Finally, Chaim Waitz testified that around noon on that day, and as he was coming home for lunch, he noticed from across the street that two Jews were running quickly out of the building in which he and the Kohns lived, in the direction of the Wood Market. It seemed to him that they were in an extraordinary rush, which drew his attention because in the previous week he had lost a cushion in his house and wanted to make sure that they were not carrying anything off from there. He could only see them from the side, however, until they turned the corner at the Bird Market into Cracow Street, when he could see them better, and his description of the taller man matched that of the previous witnesses.[13]

The police concluded from these testimonies that the man described by all of these witnesses was the person who had entered the Kohns' kitchen and committed the poisoning.

As stated previously, on the afternoon of the poisoning a number of known opponents of Rabbi Kohn were arrested for questioning, and these included one Gabriel Suchestoff. The next day, the chair and secretary of the Jewish community reported to the police that this Suchestoff lived with the gold-worker Abraham Ber Pilpel. They suggested to the police that said Pilpel may well have been the poisoner, as he matched the descriptions of all the witnesses and was known to smoke cigars, which was a rarity among the Jews,[14] and he had easy access to poison. It also was likely that he was aided and abetted in the crime by Suchestoff, who was known to be an outspoken opponent of Rabbi Kohn, and was "very bigoted."[15]

On this basis, the police inspector Johann Kolischer went to Pilpel's house to verify whether he in fact matched the description, but he was not there; his wife explained that that he had left the house at about ten o'clock that morning with an unknown Jewish woman customer, and would be home soon. Kolischer asked what kind of clothes Pilpel wore, and his wife mentioned a fur hat. But when Kolischer asked to see the hat, Mrs. Pilpel said that her husband no longer wore it, since it was worn-out. But since Kolischer had himself seen Pilpel in that hat three days earlier, he searched the house for it, and found it between the bed and the wall. He therefore brought this hat to the magistrate's office, where it was examined to see whether it had any identifying features caused by proximity to the fire on the stove in the Kohns' kitchen. On close examination, a small indentation was discovered on the hat, and it was therefore brought as evidence to the Criminal Court.

The fact that the shared description of the poisoner matched Pilpel's appearance, and that he had left Lemberg under suspicious circumstances on the afternoon after the poisoning, led the investigators to conclude that Pilpel was indeed the main suspect in the crime, and on the day of the rabbi's funeral, 8 September, he was brought into custody by Joseph Radomski with the assistance of the National Guard, and was identified by Chaim Waitz, Mindel Fischler, Rive N., Freyde Wertheimer, and Elizabeth Szostokowa as the man who had asked to light his cigar in the Waitz's kitchen and then entered into that of the Kohns' and rushed out of there. With the approval of the Criminal Court, Pilpel was formally indicted on 16 and 17 October 1848 as the murderer of Abraham Kohn, along with Joel Schorr, Israel Schramek, and Gabriel Suckestoff as accomplices.

All of these indictments, as well as the continuing investigations of Herz Bernstein, Hirsch Orenstein, Mathias Urech, and Abraham Weinreb, were substantially aided by the committee established by the Progressive Jews to assist in the investigation. This committee hired a prominent attorney to assist it in this work, and provided much of the evidence to the court, based on its own investigation as well as many anonymous tips.

The criminal investigation concluded that, before the poisoning, Pilpel had no special connection to Rabbi Kohn, except for being one of the several hundred Orthodox Jews who signed the petition calling for his removal from office. The indictment against him rested on other grounds:

a. The local burgher Carl Priester testified under oath that approximately three weeks before the Kohn family poisoning, he was at Pilpel's house to order some gold work done, and overheard a conversation between the latter and another, unidentified Jew, about Rabbi Kohn. The unidentified Jew asked Pilpel what he had against Kohn, who seemed like an honest man dedicated to improving the education of the Jews. Pilpel answered: "Kohn understands nothing about the Talmud or Jewish traditions and is unworthy of this position—*he is a dog who should be put to sleep.*"[16] (The court later found, however, that there was no legal basis to regard this as a threat, because Carl Priester was the only witness to the alleged conversation, and because he had, since the conversation was supposed to have taken place, been committed to a mental asylum, his claim could not be ratified.[17])

1. Rabbi Abraham Kohn, mid-nineteenth-century portrait (Library of Jewish Theological Seminary of America).

2. Reform Temple of Lemberg, exterior photograph, early 1930s
(Library of Jewish Theological Seminary of America).

3. Reform Temple of Lemberg, late-nineteenth-century etching of
exterior and surroundings (Columbia University Library).

Das deutsch israelitische Lemberger

4. Reform Temple of Lemberg, mid-nineteenth-century etching of interior (Columbia University Library).

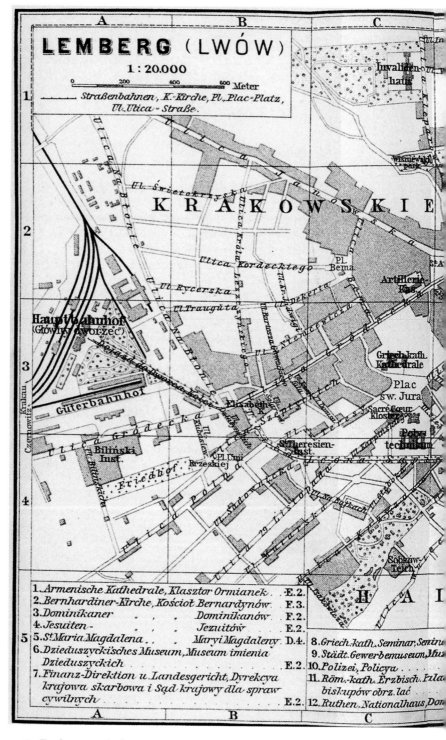

5. Early-twentieth-century map of Lemberg, with "Synagogue" at bottom

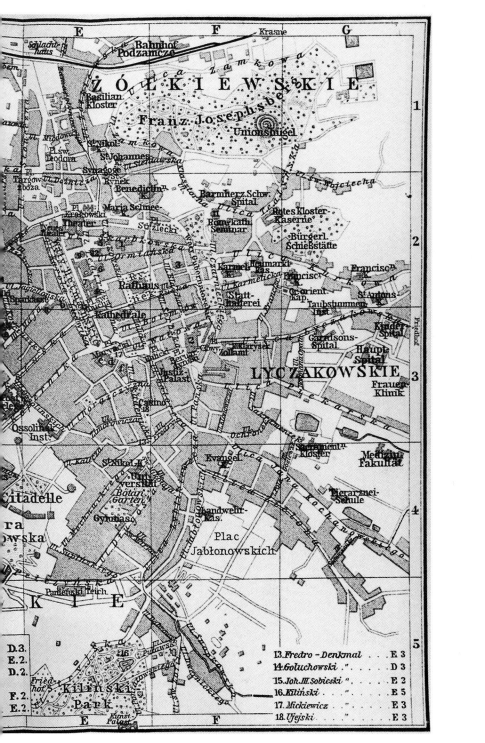

on E1, noting location of the Reform Temple (Columbia University Library).

6. Early-nineteenth-century portrait of Dr. Jacob Rappoport, one of the founders of the Reform Temple of Lemberg (Library of Jewish Theological Seminary of America).

7. Early-nineteenth-century portrait of Emanuel Blumenfeld, first president of the Reform Temple of Lemberg (Library of Jewish Theological Seminary of America).

Franz Graf Stadion, Minister.

8. Mid-nineteenth-century portrait of Count Franz Stadion, Governor of Galicia (Columbia University Library).

9. Late-nineteenth-century etching of the burning of the Lemberg Town Hall during the Revolution of 1848 (Columbia University Library).

11. Early-twentieth-century photograph of grave stone of Rabbi Abraham Kohn in the old Jewish cemetery of L'viv, destroyed by the Nazis in World War II (Library of Jew-

10. Late-twentieth-century photograph of the Jewish Hospital of Lemberg named after Dr. Jacob Rappoport, still standing in L'viv as the city's main maternity hospital (Columbia

b. Pilpel was at the site of the crime at the time of the crime: This was established by the description and statement of Mindel Fischler, who later identified him as the murderer by his figure, face, and clothing. This was confirmed by the other three witnesses, who described the perpetrator on 6 September, although when he presented himself at the police station he pretended to walk with a limp. Freyde Wertheimer, while maintaining her identification, noted that he now looked paler and spoke more slowly than on the day of the murder. She also changed her testimony about the timing of his presence in her kitchen, and now claimed to have heard his footsteps on the staircase of the Waitz residence.

c. Riva, the Waitz's cook, also identified Pilpel as the man who came into her kitchen on the day of the crime. She recognized him not only by his figure and clothes but also by his facial features and his voice, and only noted that he wore a hat at the time of the crime but was hatless at the identification.

d. Chaim Waitz also identified Pilpel by his facial features and his walk as the man he saw running away from the Kohns' house on the day of the poisoning. He swore that that there was absolutely no doubt as to this identification.

The court noted, however, that all of these witnesses had seen Pilpel before the official identification and had him described as the suspect in the murder of the rabbi. According to prosecutor Filons who was handling this case, this happened in the following manner: when Pilpel was identified as the main suspect, Filons ordered that he be sought out and arrested. He waited for Pilpel's arrival in the Town Hall, where he was conversing with the mayor, but it took some time for Pilpel to be delivered. When he arrived, Filons learned that after Pilpel had been handed over to the police by Joseph Radomski and the Jewish National guard members, one of them ran over to the Kohn/Waitz home and brought the witnesses to the magistracy to see Pilpel and identify him as the perpetrator. This was done in the presence of Attorney Menkes, hired by the committee established by the Progressive Jews to assist the investigation, and Filons officially reproached Menkes for this breach of procedure. On the next day, Filons carried out the identification process in line with standard procedure: He had the witnesses view a lineup of three Jews, including Pilpel, and all the adult witnesses immediately and without hesitation picked Pilpel out of the group as the man who entered the Waitz and then the Kohn kitchen on 6 September.[18] Only Angelica Kohn could not be certain that this was indeed the man whom she saw on that day, especially since Pilpel now looked far paler and was wearing different clothes. The Criminal Commission noted that Pilpel indeed did look far paler than he had when he was arrested.

In his rebuttal to the testimony of these witnesses, Pilpel claimed that Mindel Fischler's identification of him was a lie, caused by the actions of the Jewish National Guard in presenting him to Fischler as the culprit. This was a result of purely political factors: the National Guard were in agreement with Rabbi Kohn in taking the side of the Polish nationalists in the struggle over the future of Galicia, whereas the Orthodox Jews were loyal to the Austrian authorities. The Guard therefore sought out an Orthodox Jew to frame as the murderer of Rabbi Kohn, and settled on him as their scapegoat.[19]

He also produced an alibi as to his whereabouts at the time of the poisoning: that on 6 September he had spent the whole day, from the morning until two or three o'clock in the afternoon, at his workbench at home, completing work for the National Guard, and that one of the Guard members had come to his home to check on this work at around noon. To ratify this alibi he presented as witnesses his wife, Malka Pilpel, his apprentice Leisor Kranz, and his training apprentice Itsik Leib Kessler, as well as Ester Brat, Hersch Dittensdorf and Osias Hersh Halpern. But in the event, these witnesses could not confirm this alibi: his wife testified that she was busy with her own housework and did not notice when her husband was at home that day—alas, we have no information on why Mrs. Pilpel would incriminate her husband, if only by implication. Kranz testified under oath that Pilpel was only at work until 11 A.M. that day, and returned after 2 P.M.; and the other witnesses could not confirm Pilpel's whereabouts on the day of the poisoning.[20]

Adding to the evidence about Pilpel were the circumstances of his disappearance from Lemberg on the two days after the crime. As already noted, when the National Guard came to the Kohn house to arrest him, his wife said that he had left the home at 10 A.M. and would be back presently, but he failed to do so. Pilpel's defense was that on 7 September, between 3 and 4 P.M., a Jewish woman named Rivka Iochwed, from the village of Nawarya, came to his house asking for help in selling earrings. He went with her to try to sell the earrings, but was not success-ful, and was about to return home at about 5 or 5:30 P.M., when he ran into someone who said, "Pilpel, they're looking for you at your house." He also heard that Gabriel Suchestoff had al-ready been arrested, and that he, too, would probably be taken into custody, so he decided not to go home, but to go to Nawarja to Rivka Iochwed's house, and try to make some money there. At her home, he also received word that he was being sought by the police, made a deal with her about the jew-elry, and began to return home. But since he did not know the way back to Lemberg he got lost, and spent the night in an un-known village, and returned to the city between two and three the next afternoon, at which time he was apprehended when he appeared at a barbershop in Lemberg to get his hair cut and beard shaved, was recognized, and brought to the attention of the authorities.[21]

The court found many contradictions in this story, both re-garding Pilpel's dealings with Rivka Iochwed and with the cir-cumstances of his arrest in Lemberg, and therefore rejected the alibi as unsubstantiated, and as a result did not subject Riva Iochwed to sworn testimony. But it also rejected as unfounded the claim of the representatives of the Jewish community that Pilpel had at an earlier date committed a murder in Turkey, for which he had never been investigated or charged.[22]

The Criminal Court of Lemberg therefore formally decided, in a vote of six to two, on 24, 25, and 26 July 1849, to find Abraham Ber Pilpel guilty of the charge of murder, and sentenced him to twenty years of hard labor. Under Austrian law this was the maximum sentence possible given the circumstantial nature of the case against him. Had he confessed to the murder or had there been eyewitnesses to the crime itself, he would have been subject to the death penalty.[23] The court officially listed three grounds for this verdict:

1. The presence of the accused at the site of the crime at the time of the crime;
2. His seizure after he escaped after the crime;
3. His attempt to disguise himself after the fact by having his hair cut.[24]

All of these proceedings—the official investigation, the trial, the court's deliberations, and its verdict—took place over a period of ten months, from September 1848 to July 1849, and there is no mention in any of the court records of Pilpel's escape from prison or disappearance from Lemberg, a claim accepted as fact in the previous accounts of this case. Indeed, had he not been present at all these—and, as we shall see, at subsequent proceedings—according to Austrian law the case could not have proceeded at all.[25]

So we must conclude that contrary to previous reports, Pilpel did remain in Lemberg, and in jail, throughout this entire period. But the guilty sentence against him by the Lemberg Criminal Court did not by any means end the matter: according to Austrian criminal law, all guilty verdicts in cases regarding murder or assassination (as well as high treason, sedition, rebellion, public violence, counterfeiting, "religious troubles," duels, arson, rape, or assistance to delinquents) had to be submitted to an appellate court before they could be put into effect.[26] And so Pilpel's case was immediately appealed to the District Appellate Court of Galicia. In accord with the regnant procedure, a "*Referent*"—a specially appointed judge/investigator, here named Mochnacki, was appointed to review the case and submit a report to the appellate court.

Before proceeding with Mochnacki's official determinations, and the subsequent decision of the Appellate Court, it is crucial to emphasize the radically different political circumstances that obtained in Lemberg, and in Galicia and the Austrian Empire as a whole, in the summer and fall of 1849, as opposed to the previous autumn. Although in October 1848, Stadion and his allies in Vienna were successful in abolishing the special taxes on candles and kosher taxes incumbent on the Jews,[27] in November the Vienna authorities determined that Lemberg was still controlled by forces sympathetic to the Revolution, now deemed seditious, and as a result the city was bombarded and then occupied by the Austrian army. Martial law was introduced for Lemberg and for all of Galicia, and remained in effect until 1854.[28] Thus, when Pilpel's case came up for appeal in the summer and fall of 1849, Lemberg was in effect under the control of the Austrian army and its conservative civil appointees, including its police and court system. Within the Jewish community, this in effect meant that the Orthodox Jews of Lemberg, who had largely retained their loyalty to the Empire throughout the Revolution, were now in favor with the authorities—the reverse of the situation in the previous fall, when the case against Pilpel began. Indeed, the Orthodox Jews' regained power resulted in their success in delaying the formal appointment of a successor to Abraham Kohn as rabbi of the Temple, cynically using the argument that according to a law passed by the Habsburg monarchy in 1836 (which they had of course assiduously opposed), rabbis were required to have passed an exam administered by a university—a condition that none of the contenders for the position had fulfilled. An Orthodox rabbi acceptable to the Orenstein-Bernstein party was appointed as temporary rabbi of the community.[29]

Against this backdrop, it is perhaps not surprising that Mochnacki's report found that the third ground of Pilpel's verdict was not supportable, and the first two were questionable and had to be formally reexamined. He raised the following questions:

1. Did the interrogation of Magdalena Kohn and Mindel Fischler establish conclusively that the meat that was cooked in the soup pot was not poisoned earlier? Where was it bought? If it had a green color before it was cooked, was it sufficiently washed?

2. Is the testimony of the witnesses Mindel Fischler, Riva N., Elisabeth Szostakowa, and Freyda Werthheimer reliable as to their identification of Pilpel as the culprit? What specifics did they base their identifications on? Did they speak to him when they saw him upon his initial arrest? Was he presented to them conclusively as the murderer? Were they told that he had tried to escape from Lemberg and had tried to change his looks by cutting his hair and beard?

3. Since the accused claims that he had been in Rabbi Kohn's house three years earlier, to register his child in the metrical books of the Jewish community, is it credible that he had to ask where the rabbi lived?

4. Is the testimony of Leiser Kranz regarding the accused's presence at his place of employment on the day of the alleged poisoning credible? What is the layout of the Pilpel's house and workplace, and could Malka Pilpel, who also claimed that she was engaged in other activities that morning, have had a clear line of sight regarding her husband's comings and goings?

5. What precisely did Pilpel request from the barber on the day of his reappearance in Lemberg? Did he ask merely that his hair be cut and beard trimmed, or did he request that the latter be shaved off and his sidelocks shorn as well?

6. The establishment of the integrity of the witnesses Chaim Waitz, Mindel Fischler, Freyde Wertheimer, Riva N., and Elisabeth Szostokowa, required clarification of their political views at the time of the poisoning, and whether they were influenced in this regard by the leadership of the Jewish community.[30]

Mochnacki further emphasized that there were unresolved discrepancies beween the description of the suspect given by the witnesses and the actual appearance of Pilpel, and especially noted the inability of Angelika Kohn to identify Pilpel as the man who had entered her family's kitchen: he claimed that contrary to the ruling of the Criminal Court that an eight-year-old's testimony was not credible, "the ability of children in this age-group to identify witnesses is in fact greater than adults,"[31] and then he added that, in any event, "in general, as is well known, the identification of male Jews, all of whom wear the same type of clothing and have beards, in extremely difficult, as they all look alike."[32]

While reviewing this report, the Appellate Court was presented with a claim made by Ber Pilpel's wife and father, that Rabbi Kohn himself had declared, when he was being treated after the poisoning, that no Jew was responsible for this act. From this it must be concluded, they argued, that no murder had in fact taken place, but that Rabbi Kohn had committed suicide. Similarly, one Gedalia Herz Waschetz claimed that the rabbi had killed himself in order to avoid discovery of the fact that he had tampered with the metrical books of the Jewish community.[33] The appellate court dismissed these claims as utterly groundless.

At the same time, outraged by the lower court's decision that Pilpel had acted alone, Magdalena Kohn formally petitioned the Appellate Court to reopen the case against the other indicted co-conspirators.[34] In a few months, she would be shocked at what actually occurred.

On 29 November 1849, the Criminal Appellate Court of Lemberg issued a split decision regarding the lower court's conviction of Abraham Ber Pilpel for the murder by poisoning of Rabbi Abraham Kohn. Its four-member majority agreed with Mochnacki's claim that the case against Pilpel was not sufficiently proven: that the question of where and when the meat was purchased, and therefore when it was poisoned, had not been established; that the problems with the identifications of Pilpel by Mindel Fischler and the others rendered those identifications unreliable; that as Pilpel had in fact been at Rabbi Kohn's house to register the birth of his child, it was reasonable to question the testimony about his lack of knowledge about where precisely the Kohns lived; that Leiser Kranz was not a reliable witness; and that there were political factors that led the police and the lower court to question Pilpel's morality. One of the Court's members dissented from the last part of the decision, but concurred on the first four counts.

Therefore, the Appellate Court ruled unanimously that although it was certain that Rabbi Abraham Kohn had been poisoned, the conviction of Pilpel as the assassin of Rabbi Abraham

Kohn had not been sufficiently proven, and therefore it must be set aside, and the prisoner released.[35]

Magdalena Kohn and the entire Progressive Jewish community of Lemberg were, quite naturally, utterly outraged at this decision, and immediately appealed the decision to the highest court of the Austrian empire—the Imperial Supreme and Cassation Court.[36]

Before we follow the fate of this further appeal, let us step back and examine the cases against the other Orthodox Jews arrested in the murder of Rabbi Kohn: first, the leaders of the Orthodox community Hersch Orenstein and Herz Bernstein, and then the four Jews singled out by the police as co-conspirators with Pilpel in the actual murder.

The Indicted Co-Conspirators

BOTH appropriately and ironically, the first document in the Abraham Kohn assassination file in the archives of L'viv is a petition submitted to the Criminal Court of Lemberg on 26 September 1848 by Achse Orenstein and Witta Bernstein, the wives of Hirsch Orenstein and Jacob Herz Bernstein, supported by many other members of the Jewish community of the city, requesting the release of their husbands from jail after their arrests, three weeks earlier, in connection with the murder of Rabbi Kohn.

Despite the fact that Orenstein and Bernstein were the richest Jews in Lemberg, largely through their status as the chief tax-farmers of the Jewish community, and hence had enormous political clout both within the Jewish community and with the authorities, the Criminal Court of Lemberg rejected these appeals, on the grounds that there was sufficient evidence against the suspects to continue holding them in prison pending a thorough investigation of their role in the assassination of Rabbi Kohn.

The court based itself on accusations presented to it by forty members of the "progressive" party of Lemberg Jewry, including:

1. Orenstein and Bernstein were the heads of the party that opposed Rabbi Kohn and repeatedly tried to have him dismissed from his position as District Rabbi. They sponsored petitions to the government and gathered signatures to this effect, but were unsuccessful in disposing of Rabbi Kohn in this manner.

2. After the new constitution was promulgated, petitions against Rabbi Kohn were drawn up, which the suspects circulated in the main synagogue of Lemberg.

3. An attack was launched against Rabbi Kohn's house after a proclamation was posted in the synagogue demanding that Orenstein replace him as District Rabbi, and their alleged co-conspirator Abraham Mieses demanded that Rabbi Kohn hand over to the suspects the record books of the Jewish community. Two other co-conspirators, Joel Schorr and Elias Korpus, were involved in these excesses.

4. Shortly thereafter, a murder attempt was made against Rabbi Kohn, and Orenstein offered protection to the perpetrator of this attempt and assisted him in fleeing Lemberg.

5. Orenstein and Bernstein, with the help of District Commissioner Beutel, offered Rabbi Kohn several hundred Gulden to leave Lemberg.

6. On 9 September 1848, a proclamation acclaiming his death was posted in the synagogue under the suspects' leadership, and a demonstration against Kohn was planned.

7. On 5 September 1848, the suspects were both seen having a secret conversation, and on the day of the murder, they were caught by surprise in another such conversation, along with the alleged co-conspirator Weinberg.

8. Bernstein had a conversation with Bernhard Sternklar, in which he said that Rabbi Kohn must leave Lemberg, if not willingly then by force, and his wife said that he would give half of his wealth to get rid of Kohn.

9. Bernstein and Orenstein had many articles against Rabbi Kohn published in the local newspapers and authored all the invectives circulated in the community against him.[1]

In the event, the court found that most of these charges could not be corroborated; indeed, the most important of these claims—number 4, alleging that there had been an earlier assassination attempt against Rabbi Kohn appears nowhere else in the extant documentation.

What was clear to the court—and, in retrospect, to us—is that the leaders of the Orthodox opposition to Rabbi Kohn had—for both religious and pecuniary reasons—supported the many attempts to have him deposed as District Rabbi of Lemberg. But there was no verifiable evidence of any actions on their part to use violence or force against him, and no reliable witnesses had come forth to verify any secret conversations in regard to the poisoning of Rabbi Kohn. Nonetheless, the court decided that there was still sufficient suspicion of their complicity to keep the leaders of the Orthodox faction in prison pending further investigation, which it promised their wives would be speedy.

Which it wasn't—the case was far too complex to be disposed of quickly, and the political circumstances that surrounded it were even more confused, and constantly shifting. Just a few weeks after the denial of their wives' appeals for their release, on 5 October 1848, Orenstein and Bernstein suffered a major defeat of another sort, as the basis of their huge annual income, the candle and kosher meat taxes, were—as we have already seen—deemed unfair by the Vienna regime, and slated to be formally abolished later that fall. Count Stadion's liberal views on the Jews had gained favor in Vienna, and within a few weeks a far broader bill was passed by the parliament, effectively granting the Jews equal status in the law with Christians. But only a few weeks thereafter, in November 1848, the last gasps of the revolution played themselves out in the streets of Lemberg, as workers and their supporters put up barricades to prepare another battle against the Habsburg autocracy. Vienna responded by sending troops to Lemberg, who bombarded the city and then occupied it, and—as noted earlier—introduced martial law into the city and Galicia as a whole. Under martial law, the putative emancipation of the Jews was rescinded, along with many other reforms of the previous civil administration. Most crucially, the forces within the Galician provincial and Lemberg city administration and court system that were friendly to the progressive Jews who had supported the Revolution were gradually removed from office, replaced by personnel loyal to the counterrevolution and to the Habsburg Monarchy under the new Emperor Franz Joseph.

The repercussions of this dramatic political reversal on the case against Orenstein, Bernstein, and the other Orthodox Jews arrested as suspects in a conspiracy to murder Rabbi Kohn were critical to its disposition. But before the court could decide on the roles of Orenstein and Bernstein in the putative conspiracy to kill the Reform rabbi, it had specifically to examine and rule on the cases against three other Orthodox Jews who were said to have been working most directly under their orders: Joel Schorr, Isaac Schramek, and Gabriel Suchestoff.

Joel Schorr was a noted Hebrew publisher and leading member of the Orthodox opposition to Rabbi Kohn. Eight charges were brought against him by the representatives of the Progressive Jews of Lemberg:

1. He was reported to have been overheard (by an unidentified party) to have said "We will seek all means to kill Rabbi Kohn, and after him, other members of the Reform party in Lemberg."

2. Bermann Sterklar testified under oath that Schorr was the leader of the violent demonstration against Rabbi Kohn and the attack on his house during Passover. Schorr was said to have installed himself in a house opposite that of the Kohns, and from there to have stirred the mob on to violence, shouting, "We must drag Abraham Kohn out of his house by his feet, just as Metternich was dragged out of his," at which point Sterklar testified he pulled Schorr away from the window. He further testified that he later met Schorr on the street and noted he looked unwell; the latter responded that this was all due to his being forced to tolerate the presence of Abraham Kohn in Lemberg, and he would do anything within his means to extirpate him from the city and restore its holiness.[2]

3. Another witness, Rakhmiel Mieses (one of the leaders of the progressive party) testified that during the demonstration and attack against Rabbi Kohn, he entered the fray attempting to calm the crowd down, but could not do so due to the incitement coming from Joel Schorr, who was visible in the window of the house opposite the Kohns'. On this basis, Schorr was arrested by Governor Stadion.

4. This was corroborated by one Joseph Lazarus, who testified that during that demonstration Schorr shouted that he would have Rabbi Kohn killed, and it would be seen as an act of God.

5. One of the members of the deputation from the Jewish community, Joseph Margules, testified that soon before the murder of Rabbi Kohn, Schorr was heard to say that if Kohn did not leave Lemberg with all his possessions, he would be poisoned. Under questioning Margules later admitted that he did not hear these precise words from Schorr himself but, rather, "We will soon be rid of him," which he interpreted after the event as a threat of poisoning.

6. The head of the Jewish police force of Lemberg, Samuel Gall, testified that on 5 September 1848—the day before the poisoning—he had a conversation with Schorr about the attempt to buy off Rabbi Kohn with money. Schorr said, "We must gather money to get rid of this man, and make sure no one takes his place."

7. Another witness, Jacob Gottlieb, testified under oath that he had a conversation with Schorr several days after the demonstration in front of Rabbi Kohn's house, and Schorr said, "Yes, I was active in that demonstration because I was given money to do so, so that I could support my children, and then they will send me away on some errand soon so that I will not be around when the next step takes place."

8. Jacob Gottlieb continued: On 3 or 4 September, he had a conversation with Schorr in the presence of Hersh Meiseles, in which Schorr said, "You will see what will happen with the rabbi in a few days' time. One side will win—either he or we." But Meiseles did not corroborate this claim, stating that Schorr said that in a while it would simply become clear who would win, Kohn and his party, or his Orthodox opponents.[3]

In his defense, Joel Schorr denied all these accusations, claiming that he did in fact oppose Abraham Kohn and all that he stood for, but he had never uttered the threats attributed to him, and was not involved in, much less the leader of, the demonstration against the rabbi that led to the stoning of the windows of his flat. All the witnesses against him were supporters of the minority progressive group within the Jewish community, and decided to make a scapegoat out of him on religious and political grounds.[4]

After he completed his defense, yet another charge against him was brought forth: the claim was made by one Osias Lapter that he had come, along with Schorr, to Rabbi Kohn to obtain a marriage document required by law to be issued by the District Rabbi. Rabbi Kohn provided the document and asked for the stipulated fee, which Lapter paid, but asked the rabbi for a receipt for the sum. At this, Kohn became enraged, and called Lapter "a Polish swine"—at which Schorr said, "You came from Hohenems to be the rabbi over these 'Polish swine.'" To this, Michael Bałaban, the secretary of the Jewish community who was present at the time, added that Schorr said to Kohn "If you do not leave here immediately, I will kill you with my own hands."[5]

The court found, however, that Lapter denied this whole episode, and then added something that it had never raised before: that Rabbi Kohn himself had not included this incident in his formal complaint about threats made to him by Orthodox Jews.[6] Unfortunately, this formal complaint was never before or afterward mentioned by the court, nor has it appeared in the files of the L'viv archive!

But Schorr himself, in denying this last episode, added two other interesting twists to the story. He repeated the claims that he had opposed Rabbi Kohn because of the latter's lack of Talmudic knowledge, his preaching in the "incomprehensible German language," and his personal irreligious practice, and then added the charge that Kohn had been too close to Governor Stadion and was therefore not trusted by the Orthodox community. This is the first time in the court records that the Orthodox opposition to Stadion's role was raised, giving us further insight into the complexities of both the internal and the external politics of the Jewish community: As already noted, the Orthodox Jews of Lemberg, and Galicia as a whole, had supported the government as opposed to the rebels in the course of the Revolution of 1848, but here they were faced with the reality of the Governor of Galicia supporting the Reform District Rabbi and specifically his demand for the emancipation of the Jews, including the abolition of the special Jewish taxes. Their unprecedented quandary was compounded, Schorr further testified, by the fact that some members of the Orthodox community had tried to incite the Jewish community to stand with the nobility against the anticipated emancipation of the serfs, an act that they claimed would be contrary to Jewish economic interests. Moreover, Schorr claimed, the original copy of the declaration to this effect was brought to him by none other than Ber Pilpel! Schorr then claimed that he brought this declaration himself to the attention of Governor Stadion, in order to alert him to antigovernment actions within the Jewish community.[7]

In the event, the Criminal Court of Lemberg found that not only this episode, but all the charges brought against Joel Schorr could not be verified and accounted as punishable threats against Rabbi Kohn according to the standards of Austrian penal law. Moreover, Schorr himself had an iron-clad alibi about his whereabouts on the day of the poisoning of Abraham Kohn—his travel documents demonstrated that he was in the eastern part of Galicia, and only returned to Lemberg in February 1849. Therefore, the Court found that although Schorr was obviously a dedicated enemy of Rabbi Kohn and his brand of Judaism, there was no compelling evidence against him in the assassination case, and dismissed all the charges against him.[8]

It then set forth the charges against the next Orthodox indicted co-conspirator, Isaac Schramek, who was also known to be a sworn enemy of Rabbi Kohn, and had fled Lemberg immediately after the murder, and had to be returned there by the police after his name was raised in the investigation. The first incident involving Schramek that was brought to the court's attention was a conversation that was held in the Ex-Jesuit Garden of Lemberg on 28 August 1848, between Schramek and two other Jews. One of them asked Schramek what he had against Rabbi Kohn, who seemed to be an honest man; Schramek then put his hand on his heart, looked up to the heavens, and said "We are going to poison him."[9] Yet another witness testified that earlier that summer, he had a discussion with Schramek about the plans to pay Rabbi Kohn to leave Lemberg, during which Schramek said, "Nothing is happening with these plans since

Herz Bernstein does not want to pay the necessary 1,500 florins himself, but no one else wants to contribute to this. We therefore have to find another way to get rid of Kohn, and the only solution is to heed the Talmud's law that one can kill a heretic with poison, and we must call an assembly of 100 men to decide on this act." Finally, other witnesses testified that during the Passover attack against Rabbi Kohn, Schramek was very active in inciting the crowds and gathering signatures against the rabbi, and when he was arrested, such petitions were found in his home.[10]

In his defense, Schramek vehemently denied all these charges. But as in the Schorr case, two new elements were brought forth in this case: First, Schramek himself testified that the claim that the Talmud permitted the use of poison to kill heretics was disputed by other authorities, but attributed to the Kabbalah, and other witnesses testified under oath that Schramek had said that both Herz Bernstein and Gabriel Suchestoff know the Kabbalah better than anyone else in town, and there is also a rabbi in Sadgora who knows how to use black magic to effect such a goal, and as a result of the use of such magic, an unidentified subtenant of the tax-farmers had been led to drown himself—for unexplained reasons.[11] Second, the new preacher of the temple, Moritz Löwenthal, and its vice president, Emanuel Blumenfeld, were called by the court formally to testify as to whether the Talmud did indeed call for heretics to be killed, and they both reluctantly agreed that it did. What seems to have happened is that at the early stages of the investigation and trial, the Court was leaning toward using these matters to build a case against the indicted Orthodox Jews. But when the cases were finally decided, in late November 1849, under the control of a regime sympathetic to the Orthodox as opposed to the modernist Jews, this line of argument was dropped. The Court therefore found that the evidence only proved that Schramek was an enemy of Rabbi Kohn and progressive Judaism, and found him not guilty of the charges against him.[12]

The last case was that against Gabriel Suchestoff, the son of the respected Rabbi Naphtali Herz Suchestoffer, the head of the rabbinic court in Lemberg until his death in 1836 and himself the author of *Mazevet qodesh,* a history of the rabbinate in Lemberg.[13] Gabriel Suchestoff was very poor, and had a lost an arm during a bloodletting that went wrong. As a result of this, he became a *melamed*—a teacher of small children—a lowly position in traditional Jewish society. The charges against him began with the fact, which he admitted, that he was active in seeking out signatures for the petitions against Rabbi Kohn, and often met with Bernstein and Ornstein in this regard. But, more specifically, the father of one of his students, Zalel Goldstein, testified that one evening he asked Suchestoff what he had accomplished with all his frenzied activities against Rabbi Kohn, since the latter remained in his office as District Rabbi; Suchestoff answered "In a few days we will be rid of him."[14] Another witness, Aron Radomski, testified that on the day of Rabbi Kohn's poisoning he was at Bernstein's money-lending shop along with Suchestoff, and when the news came about the poisoning, the latter said, "Thank God, today is the day when he will croak"[15]—a statement that took on more meaning as he lived in the same building as Abraham Ber Pilpel, the main suspect in the poisoning. Moreover, other witnesses testified that several weeks before the murder, Suchestoff was in a crowd with many other Jews demonstrating against Abraham Kohn outside the government headquarters in Lemberg, and when he was asked what he had against Rabbi Kohn, he answered that he personally had nothing against him, but "Herz Bernstein paid me to be here."[16] Several weeks later, other witnesses testified, Suchestoff was selling petitions against Rabbi Kohn, and when asked why he was doing so, he answered: "They (meaning Orenstein, Bernstein and Maier Mintz) want to replace Kohn with Rabbi Sachs from Berlin, since the former preaches against usury in his sermons, and they feel insulted by this. In the documents attacking Rabbi Kohn, moreover, the Hebrew words *"yemakh shmo"*—May his name be blotted out" traditionally used regarding enemies of the Jewish people, were used. Finally, another witness, Salamon Ratz, testified that at the demonstration against the Reform rabbi, Suchestoff said that if

Magdalena Kohn v. the Austrian Empire

IMMEDIATELY after the conviction of Abraham Ber Pilpel was reversed by the Appellate Court of Galicia, Magdalena Kohn and her supporters submitted a formal petition to the highest court of the Habsburg Empire, the Imperial Supreme and Cassation Court in Vienna, requesting both a reversal of the decisions of the lower courts and the reopening of the investigation of the murder of her husband. After the indicted co-conspirators were also acquitted of any guilt in the assassination, Magdalena Kohn and her advisers added the reversal of those verdicts, too, to their appeal. Under the procedures that we have witnessed before, a special prosecuting judge was appointed to review all these cases, now the Lemberg jurist and nobleman Carl Freyherr von Pohlberg. He set about to study the massive amount of materials submitted by Kohn and her attorneys—numerous affidavits and motions, and most important, formal complaints against the Lemberg and the Galician officials who had from the start handled the case of the assassination of Rabbi Kohn.

Most boldly, Magdalena Kohn argued that the prosecutors and judges on both the lower and the appellate levels of the judicial system of Lemberg and Galicia had been bribed by Hirsch Orenstein, Herz Bernstein, and the other leaders of the Orthodox Jewish community of Lemberg to set free her husband's murderer and to relieve the other conspirators of any blame in the murder.

It took von Pohlenberg about a year to study all these materials and to submit his report to the Supreme Court, which in its turn took yet another year to issue its decision, which was published on 19 March 1851.

From the start, the language of the Supreme Court even in re-stating the facts of the murder did not bode well for the appellants. Rabbi Kohn was described as the leader of the progressive party or "intelligentsia" of Lemberg Jewry, which held a "hostile attitude to the true-believing or Orthodox" Jews, and that the intellegentsia had "forced" the Criminal Court of the city to arrest the leaders of the Orthodox Jews immediately after the events of 6 September 1848.[1] It is not difficult to read between these lines a politically and religiously based antipathy to the liberal Jews of Lemberg, in both senses of that term—the progressive Jews had hardly forced the Criminal Court to take on the case, which it did, as we have seen, on direct orders from Vienna. But this was only the first, not the last, tell-tale sign of the effect of the political leanings of the Imperial Supreme and Cassation Court on its treatment of this case.

Magdalena Kohn's appeal was summarized as consisting in the following points:

1. That the actions of the original prosecutor, Filons, were replete with procedural and substantive errors, and his brief to the court contained many misstatements of facts; all of these errors were intended from the start to support Herz Bernstein, Hirsch Orenstein, and the other Orthodox leaders suspected in conspiring against Abraham Kohn.

2. That the interrogation of the main suspects was delayed unnecessarily, despite the many compaints of the appellants, and therefore not surprisingly, did not yield any substantive results.

3. That the judges of both the Lemberg Criminal and the Galician Appellate Courts were dishonestly and secretly in cahoots with the rich Orthodox suspects, again most specifically with Orenstein and Bernstein, and the latter had bribed the District Prosecutor Wierzeyski with the sum of 4,000 florins, the special investigating judge von Pohlenberg with 13,000–14,000 florins, and the judges of the Appellate Court with an undisclosed, but significantly higher amount.

4. As a result, the Appellate Court itself ought in retrospect to be deemed dishonest, and His Imperial Majesty's Government ought to appoint a new, independent, panel composed of reliable judges, to review the investigation and the court proceedings from start to finish.[2]

On the first count, the Supreme Court totally rejected Kohn's claims. It found that Prosecutor Filons and the other investigators and prosecutors had done their jobs speedily and thoroughly, and that all claims to the contrary were tendentious and unproven. Most tellingly, it specifically singled out for defense the investigation of Bernstein and Orenstein and their imprisonment for six weeks after the assassination of Rabbi Kohn, and the finding of no evidence of their complicity in that crime.

On the second count, the Court conceded that it would have been better had all the suspects been apprehended and interrogated on the day of the crime or the next day, but this proved impossible, since several were out of town and could not be brought back to Lemberg, in some cases for months. Again revealing its biases, the Court stressed that Ber Pilpel had "voluntarily" returned to Lemberg to face arrest, which he would not have done—it assumed—had he been guilty. Moreover, the claim made by Magdalena Kohn and her supporters that Prosecutor Filons had declared that the trial had attacked the "feet" rather the "heads" of the conspiracy, was imprecise and misunderstood, to imply that he had deliberately not attempted to flesh out the role in the murder of the rich Orthodox Jews. Rather, the Court found, following von Pohlenberg, that what Filons had said was that the original trial was overwhelmed by the "feet rather than the head"—that is, that it was overwhelmed by a tremendous number of unsought and often anonymous complaints and petitions by the Jews themselves, especially members of the progressive party, and by the members of the National Guard sympathetic to them, rather than by the judicial authorities themselves.

Before dealing with the most explosive charges of bribery, the Court dispensed with the claims of the appellants that they had new evidence that was ignored by the lower and appellate courts:

a. that three witnesses—Marcus Rapp, Beer Hescheles, and Moses Hescheles—had heard Joel Schorr swear in regard to Rabbi Kohn, "I will kill him with my own hands, even if I'll be hanged for this." The Court found that there was no sustainable evidence to prove that Schorr had indeed uttered this threat, and like the other threats against Rabbi Kohn's life attributed to him, had to be dismissed as unproven.

b. Magdalena Kohn disputed the questioning of the appellate court regarding the purchase of the meat that was later poisoned in her family's soup pot, claiming that many other housewives had purchased meat from the same side of beef, but no one other than the members of her household had been poisoned. The Court found that since sixteen months had passed since the purchase of this meat, it would be impossible to confirm this claim, and so it must be dismissed.

c. Magdalena Kohn claimed that the prosecutors had misrepresented her daughter Angelica's claims regarding the identification of Ber Pilpel as the man who entered her family's kitchen on 6 September 1848—Mrs. Kohn declared that her daughter had never rescinded or doubted this identification, as the prosecutor indicated in his report. The Supreme Court found no evidence to back this claim, and in any event found that the original conviction of Pilpel was based on his positive identification by other witnesses, so that Angelica's doubts were immaterial to the ultimate disposition of the case, either its first guilty verdict, or the Appellate Court's overturning of that conviction.

On the most important charge, that of bribery, the Court responded very sharply, and with only partially muted fury: there was absolutely no evidence to sustain any of these outrageous charges against the honorable judiciary of the Austrian empire, and Mrs. Kohn had been terribly—and even dangerously— advised by her "false counselors" even to bring such charges to the highest reaches of the Habsburg government. Indeed "the groundless incriminations against the entire judicial administration and individual judges might, in the future, be in and of and themselves grounds for severe punishment."[3]

With these words, dated 19 March 1851, the file on the murder of Rabbi Abraham Kohn in the archives of the city of L'viv comes to its end.[4]

TWO FINAL IRONIES. The reader will recall that on the morning of 6 September 1848, rumors were spread in Lemberg that the Kohn family was suffering from cholera, and this led Rabbi Kohn to take the children out of the house for a public walk throughout the streets of the city to demonstrate their collective health, and Magdalena Kohn to leave the house and go shopping for the meat that formed the basis of the soup that was later poisoned. Seven years later—and four years after she lost her case in the Supreme Court of the Austrian Empire—Magdalena Kohn died of cholera, at home in Lemberg.[5] At least so far as we know, the Supreme Court's threat to prosecute her for slandering its judicial system never had any real-life consequences.

And, finally, in 1878, thirty years after the assassination of Rabbi Abraham Kohn, none other than Hirsch Orenstein became the Chief Rabbi of the city of Lemberg.[6]

Conclusion

Hirsch orenstein's accession to the rabbinate of the city of Lemberg had little effect on the temple of that city, which under the increasing Polonization that followed the reorganization of the Habsburg Empire in 1867 began to be called the "Synagoga Postępowa"—the Progressive Synagogue, and flourished as an ever-expanding stronghold of modernized Judaism in Galicia in the last decades of the nineteenth century and through the interwar years. In newly independent Poland, the Jewish community of the city—once more renamed Lwów—thrived as never before, its population numbering roughly 110,000, the third largest Jewry in Poland after Warsaw and Łódz. After the Nazi-Soviet partition of Poland in mid-September 1939, Lwów came under Soviet domination, and remained so until 30 June 1941, when the Axis armies invaded the city, renamed it Lemberg, destroyed the temple as well as most other institutions of Jewish life, and soon began to ghettoize, and then to exterminate, its Jewish population. By the time the Red Army liberated the city on 26 July 1944, only two to three hundred Jews had survived in hiding in the city and its environs.

In retrospect, it is of course impossible to know with any degree of certainty what actually transpired in the kitchen of the Kohn family on that fateful day in September 1848. Despite the fact that some of the witnesses who testified about the entry of the Orthodox Jew into the Kohn kitchen on that day were not the most reliable witnesses a prosecutor or a historian could wish for, it seems virtually certain that Abraham Ber Pilpel was indeed the man who put the arsenic into the Kohn family soup pot, and therefore that his original conviction by the Lemberg Criminal Court was correct. What precisely Pilpel's motives were is impossible to ascertain from the surviving documentation— was he was moved primarily by religious opposition to Rabbi Kohn, was he was paid to commit this heinous act, or did he act out of a combination of these two motives? Most likely, although not provable on the basis of the evidence that has so far come to light, he was merely the hired hit man in a conspiracy launched, and paid for, by Herz Bernstein and Hirsch Orenstein, who themselves were motivated by a combination of financial self-interest and religious zealotry. Certainly, there was enough credible evidence to sustain the supposition that some of the other Jews indicted as co-conspirators had been involved in the previous physical attacks against the Reform rabbi, and for the Appellate and Supreme Courts of Austria to dismiss the charges against them, and especially against Pilpel, was evidence of the utter politicization of this case in the reaction to the Revolution of 1848, rather than an objective adjudication of its facts and circumstances. Moreover, it is at least within the realm of distinct possibility that money did pass between the hands of the Bernstein-Orenstein faction and some of the local prosecutors and even judges who dealt with the case.

To be sure, some of the questions and doubts raised by the Appellate Court of Galicia and sustained by the Supreme Court of the empire regarding the guilt of Abraham Ber Pilpel and the role played in the assassination by the Orenstein-Bernstein faction seem to bear some credence—especially the crucial mistake made by the lawyer hired by the Progressive community, who allowed the witnesses to see Pilpel after he had been brought into custody but before he was presented to them in a lineup. But most of the other questions raised by the higher courts, especially the utter rejection of Magdalena Kohn's claim that others had bought the same meat and had not died from poisoning, appear in retrospect to be extremely weak, because the fact of the matter was that there were no other cases of poison-related death among the Jews of Lemberg in early September 1848, and the speculation that the meat was poisoned before being cooked

in the Kohn kitchen was thus all but nonsensical. Similarly, the
fact that Pilpel had three years earlier come to the Kohn apartment in a building that housed many other residences cannot
credibly be used to discredit his confusion about whether the
kitchen he first entered was that of the Kohn family or that of another family. And finally and perhaps most importantly, the fact
that Pilpel's coworkers and even his wife directly contradicted
his alibi about where he was at the time of the poisoning; that he
fled Lemberg immediately after that event; and that on his return, he tried to change his appearance by having his hair cut
and beard and sidelocks shaven, all point to his guilt and should
not have been dismissed as evidence by the Appellate and
Supreme Courts.

But until and unless further documentation surfaces, in the
archives of L'viv or Vienna or somewhere else, these assump-
tions about the guilt of Pilpel and the existence of a conspiracy
to kill Rabbi Kohn cannot be sustained with any proof, and so
technically the murder of Abraham Kohn must remain an un-
solved case.[1]

BUT EVEN in the unlikely event that it was another Orthodox Jew
who killed Abraham Kohn, his assassination represents a radical
new departure in Jewish history, on several fronts. First and
foremost, although we have no way of knowing the extent of internal Jewish religiously or politically based murders before
then, it seems fair to speculate that throughout the ancient, medieval and early modern periods, most religiously sanctioned
murders within the Jewish community concerned "informers"—
Jews who denounced their local communal and rabbinical leadership to the government. This problem was so prevalent in an-
tiquity that a prayer condemning informers was even included
in the *Amidah* (or "Eighteen Benedictions"), one of the central
prayers of the Jewish liturgy, recited thrice daily: "Let there be
no hope for slanderers, and let all wickedness perish in an in-
stant, may all your enemies quickly be cut down, and may you
soon in our day uproot, crush, cast down and humble the

dominion of arrogance. Blessed are you, O Lord, who smashes enemies and humbles the arrogant."[2] In the medieval period, the rabbinic laws regarding informers (*mosrim* in Hebrew) were most authoritatively summarized and codified by Maimonides, first in his laws regarding witnesses: "It was not necessary for the sages to cite informers, heretics and apostates as invalid witnesses, for they were regarded as the wicked of Israel and lower than the Gentiles, for Gentiles are not 'placed in the pit and not brought up from it,' and the righteous among them have a place in the World-to Come, while these are placed in the pit and are not brought up from it, and have no place in the World-to-Come;"[3] and then even more frontally: "It is forbidden to inform [on Jews] to Gentiles, either regarding persons or property . . . and he who does so forfeits his place in the World-to-Come. It is everywhere permissible to kill an informer even in the present time, when we do not practice capital punishment."[4]

Indeed, one of the most famous examples of the killing of informers occurred just across the border from Galicia only eight years before the assassination of Abraham Kohn: In February 1840, the entire Jewish community of the Russian Empire was roiled by the culmination of a four-year investigation of the murder of two Jewish informers in Ukraine. In February 1836, two fishermen from the village of Wonkowce in the province of Podolia had reeled in their nets and discovered a frozen body embroiled in their lines, with heavy rocks attached to the neck and legs of the corpse, which also showed clear signs of having been tortured.[5] The police started an investigation, and a well-known Jewish informer from faraway Vilnius, Isaac Kenigsberg, informed them that the frozen body was likely to be that of a local Jewish informer from the town of Ushits, Isaac Oksman, and that another Jewish informer, Shmuel Schwarzmann from the nearby town of Sokolci, had disappeared at the same time. The speculation was that both Oksman and Schwarzmann had been murdered on the order of the rabbis and lay leaders of their respective communities, as a result of their conveying information to the authorities regarding Jews' avoidance of the military conscription system.

After extensive forensic investigation it was indeed confirmed that the frozen corpse was that of Oksman, who was probably killed while traveling through a forest, and his body was then thrown into a nearby river. Schwarzmann's body was never discovered, but he was probably "strangled while praying in the Ushits town synagogue; his body was dismembered and cremated in the bathhouse furnace."[6]

Extensive military and civil proceedings then followed, in which Tsar Nicholas I himself took a personal interest, and in February 1840 concluded with the determination that the murder:

> ... had been committed as an ostensibly legal execution, according to the verdict of their courts, which was made up mostly of respected Jews and the leaders of the town of Ushits. . . . They took counsel and resolved to murder the informers. Right away they appointed murderers and personally persuaded them to carry out the plan decisively; this was not done through bribery but also for motives of mad fanaticism, citing deplorable ordinances from a few religious tomes, according to which the mutilation and assassination of an informer is the personal obligation of every Jew.[7]

Six elderly leaders of the Jewish community of Ushits were sentenced to hundreds of lashes, banished to Siberia and to terms of hard labor, others were given lesser sentences, and perhaps most remarkably, the Russian officials who had mishandled the case were fired from their positions in the imperial bureaucracy.[8]

The eight years that separate the Ushits and Lemberg cases witnessed a crucial divide between the old and the new. It is not very likely that the leaders of the Orthodox Jewish community of Lemberg viewed Abraham Kohn as an informer, even though some of the broadsheets and pamphlets attacking against him did indeed raise this charge as a result of his condemnation to the Austrian authorities of irregularities and inequities regarding the taxes on kosher slaughtering and on candles used for

ritual purposes. It is far more likely that some (or many) Orthodox Jews in Lemberg regarded Abraham Kohn simply as a
heretic, even under Maimonides's rather stringent definitions
thereof. But so far as we know, no Jewish community in medieval or early modern Europe ever ordered a heretic killed, as
opposed to excommunicated, on the basis of his or her beliefs.
Moreover, even had a charge of Rabbi Kohn being an informant
or a heretic been brought before a rabbinical court and had been
given any credence, it is impossible to imagine that such a tribu-
nal would ever authorize the killing of an entire family, including young children, for the crimes of its father.[9] (Of course, it is
possible that a rabbinic court could have authorized his murder
as an informer, but not the means of that murder, which was the
decision of the murderer himself.) But it seems prudent to conclude that even if some elements of the Lemberg Orthodox leadership did conspire to have Rabbi Kohn murdered, it is unlikely
that they sought or invoked any technical Jewish legal justification for this act.

As I have argued elsewhere and repeatedly, the assumption
that all Jews in the past based their everyday life and their actions on authoritative Jewish law or on shifting rabbinical inter-
pretations of that law, is an ahistoric retrojection, a romanticiza-
tion of Jewish life in the past that confuses the prescriptive and
the descriptive—what Jews were commanded to do and what
they actually did—as well as the historical evidence at our disposal.[10] Thus, it does not in the least strain credulity to imagine
that individual Jews in Lemberg such as Orenstein, Bernstein,
Pilpel, and Schorr, believed that killing Rabbi Kohn was an act
motivated and justified by their religious faith, and by his acts
and beliefs that they felt were threatening that faith, but that
they acted without formal rabbinic authorization. Indeed, even
without the political and financial motives surrounding the
Kohn murder, just twelve years later, a group of Orthodox Jewish youths in Amsterdam entered the Reform temple of that city,
Schochrei Deah, and stoned its rabbi, Dr. M. Chronik, almost
killing him. The Dutch authorities punished the culprits, and
one of the leading Modern Orthodox leaders of the day, Rabbi

Esriel Hildesheimer, condemned this attack as a *"hilul ha-shem,"* a profanation of God's name.[11] But to the best of our knowledge there was, alas, no comparable Orthodox condemnation of the murder of Rabbi Abraham Kohn in Lemberg, or anywhere else.

Far more generally, it is analytically both impossible and fruitless to try to distinguish between a "religious" and a "political" motivation for this assassination. As we have learned all too well, despite the Enlightenment distinction between the realms of the political and that of the religious, in real life the two are so inextricably intertwined as to be inseparable, especially in the minds of religious believers. And it is hardly a novel thought to note that religion, politics, and financial self-interest were in the past and are today, ubiquitously intertwined.

And so the assassination of Rabbi Abraham Kohn was a radical turning point in Jewish history because for the first, but alas not the last, time since the "wars of the Jews" under the Romans, do we encounter the murder of a Jewish leader by another Jew on the basis of political-cum-religious motivations. Indeed, two of the most famous twentieth-century political assassinations by one Jew of another are similar to that of Abraham Kohn in that they remain unresolved to this day, although we think we know who perpetrated them: First, the murder on 30 June 1924, of Jacob Israel De Haan, one of the leaders of the ultra-Orthodox Agudath Israel party in Palestine, outside the Sha'arei Zedek Hospital in Jerusalem after he had finished his evening prayers—generally believed to have been ordered and carried out by the Haganah in retribution for De Haan's negotiations with Arab leaders and opposition to a future Zionist state.[12] And on the other side of the political spectrum, the assassination in June 1930 of the Labor Zionist leader Haim Arlosoroff, while walking with his wife on the seashore of Tel Aviv—a crime for which three Revisionist Zionist activists were arrested, two quickly acquitted, and one, Abraham Stavsky, convicted by a lower court, but then (in an eery parallel to the case of Abraham Ber Pilpel) found not guilty by the Supreme Court of British Palestine for lack of evidence—although it is still generally believed, at least by those on the left of the Israeli political spectrum, that he was indeed responsible for the crime, whereas this is vehemently denied by those on the right.[13]

And, finally, of course, the most famous, and undoubtedly the most historically significant, political/religious assassination in modern Jewish history, that of Prime Minister Yitshak Rabin on 4 November 1995, at a peace rally in the heart of Tel Aviv. At least in this case there is no debate over who the assassin was, or his motivation—Yigal Amir, an Orthodox and extremist rightwing Zionist opposed to the prime minister's policies regarding peace with the Palestinians. Although the vast majority of Orthodox Jews in Israel and abroad abhorred Amir's actions, he and his supporters (almost exclusively from extreme rightwing groups in Israel that combine religious Orthodoxy and absolute opposition to the peace process,) continue to insist that he was working in the name of the Lord. And, all too tragically, the debate about the extent to which Jewish law permits or prohibits such murders continues to this day[14] (these words are being written in the immediate aftermath of the withdrawal of Israeli settlers and armed forces from Gaza).

Indeed, far more broadly, the Kohn assassination reveals a fundamental aspect of modern Jewish history that has heretofore remained all but unstudied: the alliance in many times and places between Orthodox (and other forms of traditionalist Jewry) and conservative and even reactionary political forces and states—even in unexpected places like late tsarist Russia, where we have just begun to understand the growing coalition that emerged between the government and the leadership of Orthodox Judaism. More well known is the alliance between the Agudath Israel party and the increasingly antisemitic government of late-interwar Poland, and we are just now beginning to have studies on such alliances in contemporary Israel, and even, most recently, in the United States as well.[15]

The fact that these alliances, and its most radical ramification—assassinations—happened in the modern period, and the Kohn murder occurred in the midst of one of the hallmarks of European modernity, the Revolution of 1848, only further reinforces our growing awareness that the old expectation that religious divides and religiously based violence would gradually diminish and disappear in the modern world, were wildly overoptimistic and, in fact, simply wrong. Whether in the Middle East, South Asia, Africa, Ireland, Great Britain, or indeed in the United States, the deadly combination of religiously and politically based murders continues to flourish and to increase, seemingly from day to day.

Afterword

THE FAMOUS HISTORIAN Marc
Bloch once remarked that anyone wishing truly to understand
the history of France must get his boots dirty with its mud. And
so, even though (as described earlier) the documents that form
the core of this book were very professionally collected for me
by archivists in L'viv, Ukraine, and sent to New York by friendly
couriers, and most of the text was written in the verdant tran-
quility of southern Vermont, as far away as possible from the
turbulence of Eastern Europe and Eastern European Jewry, I
knew from the start that to feel the story I aim to tell as well as to
write it, I had to heed Bloch's advice and get my shoes dirty
with the mud of L'viv. I therefore traveled to L'viv in possibly its
worst season—the end of December, between the Christmas
celebrated by its Ukrainian-Catholic residents and that celebrated, a fortnight later, by its Ukrainian-Orthodox faithful, and
tramped through its mud and slush in full compliance with
Bloch's dictum.

I am a seasoned traveler to the former Soviet Union and the
former Soviet bloc, and have spent many a day walking the
streets of countless cities, towns, and villages, struggling to
summon my historical imagination in order to see these places
in my mind's eye not as they appear in the present, but as they
were in the past, and particularly in the nineteenth century,
where I have lived most of my professional life. This is not the
result of any Romanticism or nostalgia on my part—merely an
attempt to see beyond the gray gloom, the shabby decrepitude,
and the shoddy neglect that characterized the Soviet Union and
Soviet-dominated Eastern Europe in the decades before the fall
of Communism. Moreover, the specific problem of trying, in the

aftermath of the Nazi Holocaust, to visualize the thriving Jewish life that was lived in these streets, in these very same cities, towns, and villages, has always been psychologically far easier for me to do far away from, rather than in Eastern Europe itself, where the absence and the erasure are almost literally palpable, and thus all but unbearable.

Slowly, very slowly, in the years after the fall of Communism, reality started to catch up with the imagined past. The gilded spires of St. Petersburg began to shine once again, the old towns of Warsaw and Vilnius were restored to a beauty they perhaps never before enjoyed, and even the countryside and its villages seemed to regain some rustic charm, even though the rush to capitalism was everywhere vulgar and crude, and cruelly dismissive of entire segments of society abandoned to perpetual poverty without even the contemplation of a safety net. Even more slowly and fitfully did the Jewish history and culture of this part of the world—for nearly half a millennium the home of the vast majority of the Jewish people—begin to be recognized, if not restored because not restorable. In some places, the Jewish past has even been highlighted and advertised abroad by the local authorities, both out of the best of reasons, and to attract Jews seeking their roots. At times, the cynical commercialism and the huge dose of kitsch involved seemed worse than the silence: who really wants to buy all those "little Jew" dolls sold in the streets of Cracow and the old town of Warsaw as ostensibly ethnographically authentic replicas of Hasidim or klezmer-players, or listen to an old man pretending to be a survivor of the Vilnius ghetto recite the Kaddish memorial prayer incorrectly, from a faded Russian transliteration, in the town's Jewish cemetery, for contributions from visiting American tourists? But as every year passes, the kitsch and the commercialism seem to diminish, and serious local scholarship on matters Jewish has grown exponentially in places where, twenty years ago, they were utterly inconceivable.

Yet even against this backdrop, I must confess I was not prepared for what I found in L'viv. Perhaps I had read too many memoirs of Jews and Poles from nineteenth-century Lemberg or interwar Lwów boasting about their beguiling, aristocratic mini-Vienna; seen too many photographs and fading filmstrips recalling its Habsburg and Art Nouveau architectural glories; spent too much time retracing the blossoming in the early and mid-nineteenth century of its middle- and upper-middle-class Jewish community and the splendid Reform temple they built, inviting as their first rabbi one Abraham Kohn, who preached with great success to hundreds of lawyers, doctors, bankers, and their families, who sought—and found—a modernized Judaism that could serve their spiritual, aesthetic, and educational needs.

Perhaps I was expecting a kinder and gentler, more gemütlich Austrian version of Riga—another city acquired by the Soviet Union in the first phase of what we call the Second World War that boasts scores of remarkable fin-de-siècle buildings and had a substantial middle-class, German-speaking, Jewish community which, already in 1840, several years before their counterparts in Lemberg, invited to their city a different reforming German rabbi, Max Lilienthal, to be their modern-style "teacher and preacher in Israel"—a story I told in my doctoral dissertation and then in my first book a quarter-century ago?[1] Consciously I knew and could lecture at length about the differences between post-Soviet Latvia and Ukraine—the former joining the other Baltic states in a thriving capitalist economy recently welcomed with open arms into the European Community; the latter a stiflingly poor, massively larger country, barely surviving in the new post-Soviet world, its frail economy far less well-known in the West than its recent political turmoil, in which its current president, poisoned by a cabal of former KGB hoods in the employ of his predecessor, rose to power in a glorious Orange Revolution we all watched breathlessly in real-time on CNN.

But the L'viv I found is not only not like Riga or Warsaw or St. Petersburg or other thriving post-Soviet cities. Most depressing to me, it is almost impossible to imagine it as interwar Lwów, not to speak of nineteenth-century Lemberg. To be fair, this is largely the result of the rank poverty of the city and of Ukraine as a whole: there is simply no money to be spent in tearing down the detritus of the Soviet years, the endless blocks of gray concrete apartment buildings erected quickly in a crazed Orwellian nightmare of civic improvement, the dream of creating a workers' paradise vitiated from the start by corruption, cynicism, ineptitude, and sheer and unrelenting ugliness. There is no money to restore the hundreds of pre-1939 buildings that survived the Nazi occupation but were left to rot away under Soviet rule, and so walking along any street in the center of the city one encounters buildings with ornate Art Nouveau decorative cornices replete with seductive nymphs and erotically charged snakes, who seem almost grotesquely to be snickering at the broken and defaced facades beneath them.

There are, to be sure, some fine old buildings in L'viv: a grand Viennese-style Opera House, resplendent at the head of an impressive boulevard that has stirringly been renamed "Prospekt Svobody"—the Avenue of Freedom; glorious cathedrals and dozens of lovely small churches, lovingly reconsecrated and restored by the four Christian denominations that have thrived (and been persecuted) in the city—Armenian, Ukrainian-Orthodox, Ukrainian-Catholic, and Roman Catholic; the main "Market Square" now under reconstruction, will in time be restored, and will again invoke the baroque and renaissance original styles of its seventeenth- and eighteenth-century merchants' townhouses still called—with almost bitter irony—by their old names: "Italian Yard," "Venice House," "Black Mansion." The remarkable Moorish blue-and-gold domed old Jewish Hospital, now L'viv's general maternity ward, still exists around the corner from the street named for its founder, Dr. Jacob Rappoport, one of the founders of the Temple of Lemberg. Here and there one comes across a beautifully restored Art Nouveau building— invariably (as in so many other places in the post-Soviet world) now occupied by a bank, an investment company, or an upscale real estate venture that cater to the city's new wealth that shops in the Mercedes-Benz and BMW dealerships and the Parisian and Milanese fashion-houses that are but steps away from open-air markets where peasants from outlying villages still bring in and spread directly on the ground their recently slaughtered chickens, skinned goats, and carefully picked apples and onions.

But almost unique to L'viv is the virtually total demographic realignment of the city, its transformation from a largely Polish and Jewish town before 1939 to an "ethnically pure" Ukrainian one today. The murder of the Jews by the Nazis was followed by the Soviets' forced "resettlement" of the local Poles to the newly acquired "Western Territories" of Communist Poland, that is, the lands seized from Germany that quite literally moved Poland hundreds of kilometers westward, Stalin's compensation for the annexation of eastern Poland and western Ukraine into the USSR. The ethnic cleansing of the Jews and the Poles was then followed by an enforced transfer of hundreds of thousands of Ukrainians from their former abodes in other parts of Poland or Ukraine into the city now renamed L'viv in Ukrainian, but in which authentic Ukrainian life was outlawed; and here they were joined by thousands of peasants from the surrounding countryside understandably eager to partake of the city's ostensible economic opportunities, and the empty flats of the former Polish and Jewish residents.

The result—quite apart from the "Jewish Question"—is radically different from the ethnic mixture that still obtains in other parts of the former Soviet Union, including Ukraine: Kiev and other cities in Eastern Ukraine still include substantial Russian populations, often to the chagrin of extreme Ukrainian nationalists who are tempted, but thankfully have not succeeded, in withholding their basic democratic rights. Alas, this is less true in other parts of the former Soviet Empire: in Vilnius, the Lithuanian authorities are deliberately and obscenely obfuscating the city's glorious Polish past—its role as the home town of both Józef Piłsudski and Czesław Miłosz, as the seat of Polish nationalism and cultural efflorescence for centuries—in sharp contrast to their eager celebration of their city's Jewish history to foreign tourists. In Talinn, I have more than once gotten into arguments with tour guides who less than twenty years ago explained to visitors from the West that in the summer of 1940, the local proletariat rose up spontaneously to beg for support from their kindly

Russian big brothers against the local fascist threat—in other words, the Red Army invaded and seized Estonia. And now, the very same guides recite a new litany that explains to the current cohort of tourists that of course Estonia cannot accord basic human rights to its Russian minority since they don't want to be part of Estonian culture! But these outrages are the result of the fact that there still is a substantial Polish population in Vilnius and a large Russian population in Talinn—minorities who can still be discriminated against, one may cynically put it, in the old local style.

But not in L'viv: there are handfuls of Jews and Poles there, the former mostly not born in the city but who found themselves there after the war, and for some reason chose not to emigrate. But there are no real Polish or Jewish (not to speak of German-speaking) communities. The helpful L'viv city tourist office can provide one with a Polish-language map of the city with the old pre-1939 street names in place—"Mickiewicz Boulevard" instead of Prospekt Svobody, "Piłsudski" Avenue instead of Ivan Franko Street (named after the most famous martyred local Ukrainian author), and a well-meaning pamphlet titled "Jewish Heritage of L'viv"—but these are at best as dizzyingly disorienting as was the German-language map from the 1910 Baedecker guide to "Austria," which I brought with me (and reproduced as Figure 5). At least for the Polish tourists the churches still survive and can be worshipped in. The Nazis made sure to destroy all the synagogues, the old cemetery, and most of the Jewish institutions of the city immediately after its occupation, and even before they ghettoized and then killed its Jews. The Ukrainian authorities have dutifully put up memorial plaques where some of the synagogues (including the Reform Temple) once stood, at the site of where the great Yiddish writer Sholem Aleichem lived for a brief period, and have erected a stirring monument to the victims of the Nazi genocide. But once again I conclude, not out of Romanticism or nostalgia but out of sheer historicist sadness, that Lwów and Lemberg no longer exist—barely even in memory.

But I do not for a moment regret heeding Bloch's advice and muddying my shoes with the slush of L'viv in late December. In addition to the necessary reality check, I was able at least to stand in contemplative silence at the site of the destroyed Reform Temple of Lemberg, just barely a few hundred meters behind the resplendent restored opera house; photograph the interwar apartment house nearby that now stands on the precise spot where the building that housed Rabbi Abraham Kohn's flat stood in 1848; visualize the direction of the stroll he took with three of his children in the hills of Lemberg on the fateful morning before he was killed; and even trace the exact escape route that his killer took, as described by a witness in the court records I described earlier.

But, most surprisingly, I came to realize that beyond what I believe are the tragic, long-lasting legacies of the murder story that I have been working on for the last few years, this book can at the same time serve a totally different, and originally unintended function: as an elegy, however complex and convoluted, to a thriving and dynamic Jewish community that was so brutally destroyed.

And so it is to all the murdered Jews of Lemberg/Lwów/ L'viv that I dedicate this little book: *yehi zikhram barukh*—may their memory be for a blessing.

Acknowledgments

Mᴏꜱᴛ Y ᴘʀɪᴍᴀʀʏ ᴅᴇʙᴛ is to Ivan Svarnyk, Head of the Sector of Auxiliary Historical Disciplines, Central State Historical Archive in L'viv. Mr. Svarnyk identified for me and had copied all the archival documents currently discoverable in L'viv relating to the case of Abraham Kohn, and through various intermediaries, especially my old friend and colleague Professor Frank Sysyn, Director of the Peter Jacyk Centre for Ukrainian Research of the Canadian Institute of Ukrainian Studies, University of Alberta, and Professor Yaroslav Hrytsak, Chair of Slavic History, L'viv State University, had these documents sent to me in New York. In addition, Dr. Rachel Manekin of the Central Archives for the History of the Jewish People in Jerusalem shared her vast expertise on the archival holdings relating to the history of the Jews in L'viv and Galicia with me, and I look forward to the appearance of her own work on the subject of Rabbi Abraham Kohn in the broader context of Galician Jewry.

As already noted earlier, I owe a huge debt to Mr. John Grossmann of New York City, and especially to Georg Vogeler and his staff at the Abteilung Geschichtliche Hilfswissenschaften Ludwig-Maximilians-Universität München for transcribing into Latin characters the archival material extant in L'viv in nineteenth-century German Gothic handwritings. My thanks go to my former student and colleague Professor Michael Brenner of Munich for putting me in touch with his colleagues. In addition, I am grateful to my former student and now colleague Professor Magda Teter for transcribing a nineteenth-century Polish document into Latin characters.

More generally, I owe a deep debt to three close friends and fellow historians who helped me with this book: Professor

David Assaf of Tel Aviv University provided bibliographic references and much needed moral support; and Professor Elisheva Carlebach of Queens College and the Graduate Center of the City University of New York and Professor Marsha Rozenblit of the University of Maryland went over every page of an early draft of this book and saved me from many errors and infelicities. At Princeton University Press, Brigitta van Rheinberg has been the most enthusiastic and supportive editor one could wish for, and I thank her and her staff for all their assistance.

Finally, as usual, my most profound gratitude is to my wife Marjorie Kaplan and our children Ethan, Aaron, and Emma, who, put as simply and clearly as I can, make my life and work worthwhile.

Notes

INTRODUCTION

1. *Encyclopedia Judaica* (Jerusalem: Keter, 1972), vol. 10, 1143. This article is signed "M. Lan"—the abbreviation for Moshe Landau, identified as an "educator in Tel Aviv" in the Index volume, 60. The article on L'viv itself (under the 1972 name of the city, L'vov) is hardly more accurate, though from a seemingly different ideological perspective: "he and his family were poisoned and Orthodox fanatics were accused of having committed the crime" (vol. 11, 612). This article is signed "A. Ru" for Avraham Rubinstein, then a Senior Lecturer in Jewish History at Bar Ilan University.

2. The most extensive treatment of the subject to date is in Majer Bałaban, *Historia lwowskiej synagogi postępowi* (Lwów: Nakładem Zarzadu synagogi postępowei we Lwowie, 1937), a commissioned history of the Lemberg Temple by the foremost contemporary historian of Polish Jewry, murdered in the Holocaust five years later. It is not clear to me whether Bałaban had access to the court documents I use here, since he does not allude to them, and as we shall see, provides incorrect information, later repeated by many authors, about Ber Pilpel's ultimate escape from Lemberg (from what source I do not know).

CHAPTER ONE: GALICIA AND ITS JEWS, 1772–1848

1. Norman Davies, *God's Play Ground: A History of Poland*, vol. 1 (New York: Columbia University Press, 1982, 145.

2. Interestingly, the Jewish population acorss the border in the Russian Empire had an infant mortality rate far lower than that of the non-Jews, resulting in an even more robust population growth over the course of the nineteenth century.

3. William O. McCagg, *A History of Habsburg Jews, 1670–1918* (Bloomington: Indiana University Press, 1989), 110.

CHAPTER TWO: LEMBERG AND ITS JEWS, 1772–1848

1. Yaroslav Hrytsak, "Lviv: A Multicultural History through the Centuries," in John Czapicka, ed., *Lviv: A City in the Crosscurrents of Culture*, Harvard Ukrainian Studies, vol. xxiv (Cambridge: Ukrainian Research Institute, 2000), 50.

2. John Czapicka, "Lviv, Lemberg, Leopolis, Lwów, Lvov: A City in the Crosscurrents of European Culture," in Ibid., 23.

3. Ibid., 50–54.

4. Ibid., 53.

5. Ibid., 54.

6. Waclaw Wierzbienic, "The Processes of Jewish Emancipation and Assimilation in the Multiethnic City of Lviv during the Nineteenth and Twentieth Centuries," in Czaplicka, John, *Lviv: A City in the Crosscurrents of Culture*, Harvard Ukrainian Studies, vol. xxiv (Cambridge: Ukrainian Research Institute, 2000), 224.

7. Salo Wittmayer Baron, "Ghetto and Emancipation," *Menorah Journal* 14 (1928) 515–526.

8. Wierzbienic, "The Processes" 225. Either he or the editors of this volume, usually very careful about emphasizing the multiethnic character of the city, here anachronistically use "Lviv" rather than Lwów in the translation of this quote from a Polish-language source. I have therefore restored the original in square brackets.

9. Ibid., 225.

10. See Magda Teter, *Jews and Heretics in Catholic Poland: A Beleaguered Church in the Post-Reformation Era* (New York: Cambridge University Press, 2006).

11. Wierzbienic, "The Processes" 225.

12. Ibid., 226.

13. See Hayyim Natan, Dembitzer, *Kelilat yofi: Kolel toldot ha-rabanim be-'ir Lvov* (reprint New York: Zeev, 1959).

14. For the best sythetic view of Frankism, see Gershon Scholem, "Redemption through Sin," in his *The Messianic Idea in Judaism* (New York: Schocken Books, 1995), 78–141.

15. N. M. Gelber, ed., *Lvov* (Jerusalem and Tel-Aviv: Enziklopediah shel galuyot, 1956), 222; see Chone Shmeruk, "Mashma'auta ha-hevratit shel hashehitah hehasidit," *Mehkarim betoldot yisrael ba'et hahadashah* 1 (1995), 161–186.

16. Zvi Karl, "Lvov," *Arim ve-imahot be-yisrael*, vol. 1. (Jerusalem: Mosad Harav Kook, 1946), passim.

17. It is both impossible and naïve to attempt to separate between the intellectual and material incentives to the attraction of secular studies and the Enlightenment movement among the Jews of Lemberg or anywhere else. Just as in our day, we are dealing here with complicated human beings whose motivations cannot be defined or delimited by such categorizations or generalizations,

however attractive the latter have been to ideologues, especially those who have tried, in line with rather crude notions of Marxism, to equate the Haskalah with the rise of a putative capitalist class in Berlin, Galicia, and even in the Russian empire. For an outdated Marxist view, see Raphael Mahler, *Hasidism and the Jewish Enlightenment: Their Confrontation in Galicia and Poland in the First Half of the Nineteenth Century*, translated from the Yiddish by Eugene Orenstein; translated from the Hebrew by Aaron Klein and Jenny Machlowitz Klein (Philadelphia: Jewish Publication Society of America, 1985).

18. See, for example, Joseph Davis, "The 'Ten Questions' of Eliezer Eilburg and the Problem of Jewish Unbelief in the 16th Century," *Jewish Quarterly Review* 91 (3–4) 2001, 293–336. I am indebted to Professor Elisheva Carlebach for this reference.

19. But, as the question is being posed more and more in the scholarship, we are learning more about women adherents of the Haskalah; see Carole Balin, *To Reveal Our Hearts: Jewish Women Writers in Tsarist Russia* (Cincinnati: Hebrew Union College Press, 2000).

20. Gelber, *Lvov*, 217.

21. Ibid., 217–218.

22. Steven Lowenstein, *The Berlin Jewish Community: Enlightenment, Family, and Crisis, 1770–1830* (New York : Oxford University Press, 1994).

23. See Benedict Spinoza, *Theological-Political Treatise*, translated by R. Elwes (Indianapolis: Hackett, 2001); and Moses Mendelssohn, *Jerusalem*, translated Alan Arkush (Waltham MA: Brandeis University Press, 1983).

24. Gelber, *Lvov*, 218.

25. Ibid., 219. Because rabbis do not actually employ the power to force Jewish males to grant divorces to their wives—leading, inter alia, to the huge problem of so-called chained wives (*agunot*) in every Jewish society, it is unclear whether this rumor was grounded in reality.

26. Ibid., 226.

Chapter Three: A Reform Rabbi in Eastern Europe

1. By far the best treatment is in Michael Meyer, *Response to Modernity: A History of the Reform Movement in Judaism* (New York: Oxford University Press, 1988), 156–163, updated in his article "Religious Reform," in *The YIVO Encyclopedia of Jews in Eastern Europe*, now available only online at http://www .yivo .org.

2. With the one important, but idiosyncratic, exception of the short-lived lay "Verein der Reformfreunde" (Society of the Friends of Reform) founded in Frankfurt in 1842, which went so far as to advocate the abolition of circumcision for Jewish men—a position rejected by even the radical wing of Reform rabbis anywhere. See Meyer, 122–123.

3. Ibid., 146–151.

4. See Alexander Guterman, "The Origins of the Great Synagogue in Warsaw on Tłomackie Street," in W.T. Bartoszewski and Antony Polonsky, *The Jews in Warsaw* (Oxford, 1991), 181–210. This article, based on the author's dissertation at the Hebrew University of Jerusalem, is very helpful, but is terribly flawed by the author's use of the (albeit conventional) term "assimilationists" to describe the supporters of this synagogue—resulting in sentences such as "Most of the congregation, although, belonged to the first generation of assimilationists and were not yet prepared to give up the old, sanctified prayer forms . . ." (184). How this term can have any meaning in this context is extremely problematic; on this entire problem, see my *Zionism and the Fin de Siecle* (Berkeley: University of California Press, 2003), Chapter 1.

5. Meyer, 150. Mannheimer, like the founder of neo-Orthodox Judaism Rabbi Samson Raphael Hirsch in the beginning of his career, attempted also to eliminate the *Kol Nidre* prayer introducing Yom Kippur, but given the sanctity attributed to this prayer to Jews throughout the Ashkenazi world, this attempt was largely unsuccessful—despite the substantial halachic problems that it presented.

6. See Meyer, *Response to Modernity* 42, 60–61.

7. Bałaban, *Historia Iwowskiej*, 18–20.

8. See *The Memoirs of Ber of Bolechow (1723–1805)*, translated from the original Hebrew manuscript with an introduction, notes, and a map by M. Vishnitzer (New York: Arno Press, 1973).

9. See Samson Raphael Hirsch, *Nineteen Letters* (Jerusalem and New York: Feldheim Publishers, 1995), chapter on "Emancipation."

10. See Julian J. Busgang, "The Progressive Synagogue in Lwów," *Polin* 1 (1998), 134–135.

11. Gotthilf Kohn, *Abraham Kohn im Lichte der Geschichtsforschung: Historische Studie, verfasst zum 50-sten Gedenkjahre des Todes des Rabbiners* (Zamarstynow bei Lemberg: Im Selbstverlage des Verfassers, 1898), 13. Henceforth GK.

12. Aron Tänzer, *Die Geschichte der Juden in Hohenems* (Bregenz: Lingenhöle, 1982), 595.

13. GK, 15.

14. Ibid., 17.

15. Ibid., 17–18.

16. Tänzer, *Die Geschichte der Juden*, 598.

17. Jakob Kohn, *Leben und Wirken Abraham Kohns* (Lemberg: Poremba, 1855).

18. See Chapter Two, note 6.

19. Tänzer, *Die Geschichte der Juden*, 606.

20. See Jacob Katz, *Tradition and Crisis: Jewish Society at the End of the Middle Ages*, translated and with a afterword and bibliography by Bernard Dov Cooperman (New York: New York University Press, 1993), and Ismar Schorsch,

"Emancipation and the Crisis of Religious Authority: The Emergence of the Modern Rabbinate," in Werner Mosse et al., eds., *Revolution and Evolution: 1848 in German-Jewish History* (Tübingen: Mohr, 1981), 205–248.

21. Published by M. J. Landau and approved by the censor Karl Fischer. Henceforth SP.

22. Ibid., 4.

23. Ibid., 17.

24. See Tänzer, *Die Geschichte der Juden*, 608; the book was entitled *Petakh sefat ever.*

25. *Biblische Geschichte für die israelitische Jugend mit entsprechenden Bibelversen von jeder Erzählung* (Lemberg: Poremba, 1854); and *Chanoch-l'naar: Elemente des ersten Religions-Unterrichtes für die israelitische Jugend* ("Teach Your Children: A Primer for the Teaching of Religion to Jewish Children (Lemberg: Poremba, n.d.).

26. "Ueber die jüdischen Trauergebräuche," WZfjT 1837, 2, 214–233; "Ueber das Entbehren lederner Schuhe am Versönungstage," Ibid., 1839, 2, 165–176; "Ueber Musik an Feiertagen," Ibid., 176–185; and "Noch ein Wort über das Haartragen der Frauen," Ibid., Heft 3, 333–345.

27. Ibid., 225.

28. Ibid., 342.

29. Tänzer, *Die Geschichte der Juden*, 610.

CHAPTER FOUR: RABBI ABRAHAM KOHN IN LEMBERG, 1843–1848

1. Archives of the Jewish Community of Lemberg, Fond 2, unnumbered file, July 23, 1843, Hebrew in original. Only the latter part of the document is cited by Bałaban, 33.

2. There is some confusion here about the date of the sermon: the announcement clearly reads "parshat va-ethanan," which was read on Saturday, 19 August 1843. Bałaban *Historia lwowskiej*, (Ibid., 34) dates this to August 18, which was a Friday, and misstates the Torah portion as that of the previous Sabbath—Ekev.

3. An undated document in the Kohn file in the L'viv archives (Kohn file p.18), lists Rabbi Kohn's salary as 600 Gulden "als Rabbiner," but also another 1,500 for his services in the school and as Preacher, for a total of 2,100 Gulden per annum.

4. I have here summarized and combined the two different versions of the contract that are extant in the municipal archives, the unnumbered file, and in Bałaban, *Historia lwowskiej*, 34–35. I surmise that the archival document is a later copy of the original, which Bałaban had access to.

5. Tänzer, *Die Geschichte der Juden*, 613. I have retained the transcription of the Yiddish used in the original.

6. Bałaban, *Historia lwowskiej*, 39.

7. Piotr Wandycz, *The Lands of Partitioned Poland, 1795–1918* (Seattle: University of Washington Press, 1974), 133.

8. Ibid., 135.

9. Ibid., 134.

10. Davies, *God's Playground*, 148.

11. Gelber, *Lvov*, 239.

12. Bałaban, *Historia lwowskiej*, 265–273. This sermon was later published as a separate pamphlet entitled *Predigt gehalten bei der Einweihungs des Deutsch-Israelitischen Bethauses in Lemberg am 18. September 1846 Abends von Abraham Kohn, Religionsweiser und Prediger der Israeliten-Gemeinde.*

13. Neither Bałaban nor Gelber give the date of this appointment, but I have found it in the court records relating to the later murder of Rabbi Kohn, N.29181/1246.

14. GK, 106.

15. Gelber, *Lvov*, 242.

16. See Michael Silber, "*The Emergence of Ultra-Orthodoxy; the Invention of a Tradition,*" in Jack Wertheimer, ed., *The Uses of Tradition* (New York: Jewish Theological Seminary of America, 1992), 23–84.

17. The memo is marked No. 295 in the L'viv Archives, and a copy of it can be found in the Central Archives of the History of the Jewish People in Jerusalem, under #HMZ/8284.7. See also Gelber, *Lvov.* On the Galician Haskalah in general, see now Nancy Sinkoff, *Out of the Shtetl: Making Jews Modern in the Polish Borderlands* (Providence: Brown Judaic Studies, 2004).

18. *Ein Word zu Zeit. Gutachten über die Verhältnisse und Uebelstende der Galizischen Jude in Folge einer löblichen K.K. Kreisamtlichen Aufferderung von V . . . v. M . . . tz.*

19. Ibid.

CHAPTER FIVE: REVOLUTION AND MURDER

1. On Stadion, see the literature cited in Magocsi, 127, note 43.

2. Wandycz, *The Lands*, 142.

3. Ibid., 144.

4. Wierzbienic, "The Processes," 230.

5. Filip Friedman, *Die galizischen Juden in Kampfe um ihre Gleichberechtigung (1848–1868)* (Frankfurt am Main: Kaufmann Verlag, 1929), 56.

6. GK, 190–193.

7. Bałaban, *Historia lwowskiej*, 53, and Gelber, *Lvov*, 257. The sources often confuse the two attacks on Rabbi Kohn, that of January and April 1848. I have tried to keep the chronology straight, but the relevant police reports have not yet surfaced in the archives to insure the accuracy of any account.

8. *Offendes Sendschreiben an die Petitionäre und sogenannten Verfechter des Orthodoxen Judentums gegen den Herrn Kreisrabbiner Abraham Kohn in Lemberg.*

9. *Einige Worte an die Unterzeichneten der Petition Betreff der Entfernung des Kreisrabbiners Abraham Kohn.* Both of these are summarized, with highly pejorative editorializing in GK, 208–246. On the basis of a close reading of the language of these brochures and previous petitions penned by Meir Mintz, the moderate maskil who was steadfastly opposed to Rabbi Kohn and friendly with the Orthodox leadership, Friedman speculates that these brochures were written by Mintz himself. See his *Die galizischen Juden*, 61.

10. Ibid., and Gelber, *Lvov.*

11. A.Z. Eshcoly, "Rezah Harav Avraham Kohn z"l," *Davar* 11.6.34, p. 6. I thank my friend Professor David Assaf for this reference as well as that of the dissertation referred to in note 28.

12. Gelber, *Lvov*, 255.

13. GK, 196.

14. Ibid., 273–274.

15. Bussgang, "The Progressive Synagogue," 138.

16. Later published as Dr. E. Blumenfeld, *Worte an der Leiche des seligen Rabbiners Abraham Kohn, gesprochen in israelitischen Tempel am 8 September l.J.* (Lemberg: Poremba, 1848). The sermon given the next Saturday in the Lemberg Temple, in memory of Rabbi Kohn, was also published: Moritz Löwenthal, *Mazevet Ya'akov: Des Glaubens-Denkmal Jacobs, als Grabes-Denkmal des hochseligen Abraham Kohn, Kreisrabbiners und Predigers in Lemberg* (Lemberg: Shnayder, 1849).

17. Bałaban, *Historia lwowskiej*, 276–279.

18. Ibid., 65, and Gelber, *Lvov*, 264.

19. Ibid., 274–275.

20. McCagg, 114.

21. Cited in Eshcoly, "Razah Harav."

22. Bussgang, "The Progressive Synagogue," 138.

23. Gelber, *Lvov*, 264.

24. Encyclopedia Judaica (Jerusalem: Keter, 1972), vol. 10, 1143. This article is signed "M. Lan"—the abbreviation for Moshe Landau, identified as an "educator in Tel Aviv." Index, 60.

25. Zvi Karl, in *Arim ve-imahot be-yisrael*, vol. 1 (Jerusalem: Mosad Harav Kook, 1946), 334.

26. Zvi Karl, "The Religious Life of the Jews of Lemberg" (Hebrew), *Entsiklopediah shel galuyot*, vol. 4 (Jerusalem-Tel Aviv, 1956), 438.

27. See sources cited in Chapter One, note 8. Following the scholarship available to him, Michael Meyer in his *Response to Modernity* writes "Finally, one day a poor Jewish goldsmith, *hired for the task* (my emphasis), entered the Kohn kitchen. . . . A few days later the forty-one-year-old Kohn," 157. As we shall see, there is no evidence that Ber Pilpel was hired for the task, and, as already noted, Kohn died the day after the poisoning.

28. Eshcoly, "Rezah Harav," 10–12.

29. Reproduced in GK, 266–270.

30. Balaban, *Historia lwowskiej*, 63–65, and Gelber, *Lvov*, 263–264. Magdalena Kohn's letter to Berhard Kohn and the newspaper reports are reproduced in GK, 266–275. The question of why Hasidim should have been so concerned about the honor of Rabbi Orenstein, who had earlier excommunicated them as heretics, is never raised or examined. See also Haim Gartner, "Rabanut ve-dayanut be-Galitsiyah be-mahazit ha-rishonah shel ha-meah ha-19: Tipologiyah shel hanhagah mesoratit be-mashber," unpublished Ph.D. dissertation, Hebrew University of Jerusalem, 2004, 34–38.

Chapter Six: Abraham Ber Pilpel, Murderer?

1. See bibliography for the additional archival materials, some of which I have already cited in earlier chapters.

2. As I mention in my acknowledgments, I am grateful to Mr. John Grossmann of New York City and especially to Georg Vogeler and the staff of the Abteilung Geschichtliche Hilfswissenschaften Ludwig-Maximilians-Universität München for transcribing this material into Latin characters. It is with absolutely no disrespect to note that even the latter, among the world's experts in nineteenth-century German paleography, found 706 places in these 202 pages that were problematic and either had to be corrected or left with their meaning unresolved. In addition, there is one document in Polish, relating to the stipend raised for Magdalena Kohn and her family after the murder of Abraham Kohn. I am grateful to my colleague Magda Teter for transcribing this document for me into Latin characters.

3. I will cite the file as AK, followed by the page number.

4. AK, 29.

5. See Victor Foucher, *Code pénal général de l'empire d'Austriche* (Paris: Imprimerie Royale, 1833), chapter xvi—"Du Meurtre et de l'Homicide." Article 118 (p. 41) lists the four different types of murder defined by Austrian criminal law; the first is "L'assassinat qui se commet à l'aide du poison, ou pars d'autres moyens dissimulés."

6. AK, 30.

7. Ibid., 34.

8. Ibid., 36.

9. Ibid., 37.

10. Ibid., 38.

11. Ibid., 41.

12. Ibid., 42.

13. Ibid., 47.

14. Ibid., 48.

15. Ibid.

16. In original underscored: *"er seÿ ein Hund und soll krepiren."* Ibid., 54.

17. Ibid.

18. Ibid., 61–64.

19. Ibid., 65–68.

20. Ibid., 68–71.

21. Ibid., 71–78.

22. Ibid., 78–81.

23. Ibid., 82, and see Foucher, *Code penal*, article 430, p. 156.

24. AK, 82.

25. Foucher, *Code penal*, chapter xv.

26. Ibid., Article 433, p. 157.

27. Gelber, *Lvov*, 265.

28. Wandycz, *The Lands*, 150.

29. Zvi Karl, "Religious Life of the Jews in Lvov," 426.

30. AK, 85–92.

31. Ibid., 94.

32. Ibid., 95 (*Ueberhaupt ist die Annerkenung bei männlichen Juden, welche bekanntlich ganz gleichen Tracht haben und welche auch sonst der bart Einen den Andern änlich macht, sehr schwer*).

33. Ibid., 25.

34. Ibid., 24.

35. Ibid., 127–129.

36. Ibid., 142.

CHAPTER SEVEN: THE INDICTED CO-CONSPIRATORS

1. AK, 1–8.

2. Ibid., 99–101.

3. Ibid., 100–107.

4. Ibid.

5. Ibid., 108.

6. Ibid., 109.

7. Ibid., 111.

8. Ibid., 112–113.

9. Ibid., 115.

10. Ibid., 116–119.

11. Ibid., 118.

12. Ibid., 120.

13. The title page of the work has his name transliterated as Gawril Suchestow, *Mazevet qodesh: Hu zikhron zadikim, sefer zikaron lekhol hageonim vehaqedoshim bevet mo'ed lekhol hai po 'ir L'vov* (Lemberg: Matfes, 1863).

See also Reuven Margaliot, "Rabanim verashei-yeshivot," in Gelber, *Lvov,* vol. 4, 415.

14. AK, 121.
15. *"denn heute ist die Zeit daß er krepire."* Ibid., 122.
16. Ibid., 124.
17. Ibid., 125–127.
18. See pp. 111–111.
19. AK, 138–141.

CHAPTER EIGHT: MAGDALENA KOHN V. THE AUSTRIAN EMPIRE

1. AK, 153.
2. Ibid., 154–156.
3. AK, 190–202.
4. Ibid., 202.
5. Tänzer, *Die Geschichte der Juden,* 623, note 1.
6. Margaliot, "Rabanim ve-rashei yeshivot," 418.

CONCLUSION

1. There is the possibility that Pilpel, as a goldsmith, had easy access to arsenic, as gold-mining produces arsenic as a by-product, and hence there are several pending cases before courts in many countries accusing gold mines of polluting nearby rivers and streams with arsenic. But I have been unable to locate any sources linking the craft of goldsmiths to the use of arsenic, and the latter was used widely for medicinal purposes in nineteenth-century Eastern Europe and thus was far more easily available than it is today.

2. This so-called "Birkat ha-minim" has variously been interpreted as a prayer against Jewish Christians, apostates, and heretics, but may originally have been aimed at informers, as it was interpreted by the majority of Jewish exegetes in the medieval and modern periods. See Ismar Elbogen, *Jewish Liturgy: A Comprehensive History* (Philadelphia: Jewish Publication Society; New York: Jewish Theological Seminary of America, 1993), passim.

3. *Mishneh Torah,* Hilkhot Edut, 11:10.
4. Ibid., Hilkhot Hovel umazik 8: 9–10.
5. See David Assaf, *The Regal Way: The Life and Times of Rabbi Israel of Ruzhin* (Stanford: Stanford University Press, 2002), 109.
6. Ibid., 110.
7. Ibid., 113.
8. Ibid., 113–114.

9. I owe this crucial insight, and the reference in footnote 10, to my close friend and colleague Professor Elisheva Carlebach.

10. See my *Autobiographical Jews: Essays in Jewish Self-Fashioning* (Seattle: University of Washington Press, 2004), passim.

11. See David Ellenson, *Rabbi Esriel Hildesheimer and the Creation of a Modern Jewish Orthodoxy* (Tuscaloosa: University Alabama Press, 2003), 38.

12. See Shlomo Nakdimon and Shaul Mayzlish, *De Haan: Ha-rezah hapoliti harishon beerez yisrael* (Tel Aviv: Modan, 1985) and Shimon Rubinstein, *Shmonim shanah lehahlatat bet hadin hasodi hameyuhad shel ha-"Haganah" ladun lemavet et Yaakov De-Haan* (Jerusalem: private offprint, 2004). For ultra-Orthodox apologetic treatments of the subject that do not mention his homosexuality, see David Halevi, *Rezah be-yerushalayim* (Jerusalem: Tefuzah, 1983), and Zvi Moshe-Zahav and Yehudah Meshi-Zahav, *Ha-qadosh: Rabi Ya'aqov Yisrael De-Haan* (Jerusalem: Mahon hayahadut haharedit, 1996).

13. See Shabtai Tevet, *Rezah Arlozorov* (Jerusalem: Schocken, 1982) for the Labor Zionist version of the story, and Yosef Nedavah, ed., *Ha-neesham hasheni: maavako shel Tsevi Rozenblat le-gilui ha-emet* (Tel-Aviv: Jabotinsky Institute, 1986), for the rightwing Zionist version.

14. On political assassinations by Jews in Mandatory Palestine, see Nachman Ben-Yehudah, *Political Assassinations by Jews: A Rhetorical Device for Justice* (Albany: State University of New York Press, 1993), and for an update following the Rabin assassination, his "One More Political Murder by Jews," in Yoram Peri, ed., *The Assassination of Yitshak Rabin* (Stanford: Stanford University Press, 2000), 63–95.

15. See my recent "Reflections on the Russian Rabbinate," in Jack Wertheimer, ed., *Jewish Religious Leadership: Image and Reality* (New York: Jewish Theological Seminary, 2004), vol. 1, 429–446; and Gershon Bacon, "The New Jewish Politics and the Rabbinate in Poland: New Directions in Interwar Poland," in that volume, 447–480.

AFTERWORD

1. Michael Stanislawski, *Tsar Nicholas I and the Jews* (Philadelphia: Jewish Publication Society, 1983).

Bibliography

PRIMARY SOURCES:

Archives

L'viv: Central State Archive of the Ukrainian Soviet Socialist Republic in the city of L'vov, Department of the Supreme District Court of L'vov, Appellate Division, entitled "Case of the Accused in the Murder of Abraham Kohn," opened in 1848 and closed in 1851.

Archives of the Jewish Community of Lemberg, Fond 2, unnumbered file, July 23, 1843.

Jerusalem: Central Archives of the History of the Jewish People in Jerusalem, #HMZ/8284.7

Published Sources

Blumenfeld, Dr. E. *Worte an der Leiche des seligen Rabbiners Abraham Kohn. gesprochen in israelitischen Tempel am 8 September l.J.* Lemberg: Poremba, 1848.

Foucher, Victor. *Code pénal général de l'empire d'Austriche.* Paris: Imprimerie Royale, 1833.

Kohn, Abraham. *Biblische Geschichte für die israelitische Jugend mit entsprechenden Bibelversen von jeder Erzählung.* Lemberg: Poremba, 1854.

Kohn, Abraham. *Chanoch-l'naar: Elemente des ersten Religions-Unterrichtes für die israelitische Jugend.* Lemberg: Poremba, n.d.

Kohn, Abraham. "Noch ein Wort über das Haartragen der Frauen." *Wissenschaftliche Zeitschrift für jüdische Theologie,* 1839, Heft 3, 333–345.

Kohn, Abraham. *Petakh sefat ever.* Smyrna, 1841.

Kohn, Abraham. *Predigt gehalten bei der Einweihungs des Deutsch-Israelitischen Bethauses in Lemberg am 18. September 1846 Abends von Abraham Kohn, Religionsweiser und Prediger der Israeliten-Gemeinde.* Lemberg, 1846.

Kohn, Abraham. *Sechs Predigten gehalten in der Synagogue zu Hohenems von dortigen Rabbiner Abraham Kohn.* Prague: M. J. Landau, 1834.

Kohn, Abraham, "Ueber das Entbehren lederner Schuhe am Versönungstage," *Wissenschaftliche Zeitschrift für jüdische Theologie,* 1839, 2, 165–176.

Kohn, Abraham. "Ueber die jüdischen Trauergebräuche," *Wissenschaftliche Zeitschrift für jüdische Theologie* 1837, 2, 214–233.

Kohn, Abraham,"Ueber Musik an Feiertagen," *Wissenschaftliche Zeitschrift für jüdische Theologie*. 1839, 2, 176–185.

Löwenthal, Moritz. *Mazevet Ya'akov: Des Glaubens-Denkmal Jacobs, als Grabes-Denkmal des hochseligen Abraham Kohn, Kreisrabbiners und Predigers in Lemberg.* Lemberg: Shnayder, 1849.

Maimonides, *Mishneh Torah:* Hilkhot Edut, 11:10; Hilkhot Hovel umazik 8: 9–10.

SECONDARY MATERIALS CITED

Assaf, David. *The Regal Way: The Life and Times of Rabbi Israel of Ruzhin.* Palo Alto: Stanford University Press, 2002.

Bacon, Gershon. "The New Jewish Politics and the Rabbinate in Poland: New Directions in Interwar Poland," in Jack Wertheimer, ed., *Jewish Religious Leadership: Image and Reality.* New York: Jewish Theological Seminary, 2004, vol.1, 429–446.

Bałaban, Majer. *Historia Lwowskiej synagogi postępowei.* Lwów: Nakładem Zarzadu synagogi postęwei we Lwowie, 1937.

Balin, Carole. *To Reveal Our Hearts: Jewish Women Writers in Tsarist Russia.* Cincinnati: Hebrew Union College Press, 2000.

Baron, Salo Wittmayer. "Ghetto and Emancipation." *Menorah* 14 (June 1928): 515–526.

Ben-Yehuda, Nachman. "One More Political Murder by Jews," in Yoram Peri, ed., *The Assassination of Yitshak Rabin.* Palo Alto: Stanford University Press, 2000, 63–95.

Ben-Yehudah, Nachman. *Political Assassinations by Jews: A Rhetorical Device for Justice.* Albany: State University of New York Press, 1993.

Bolechower, Ber. *The Memoirs of Ber of Bolechow (1723–1805),* translated from the original Hebrew ms. with an introduction, notes, and a map by M. Vishnitzer. New York, Arno Press, 1973.

Busgang, Julian J. "The Progressive Synagogue in Lwów," *Polin* 1 (1998), 134–135.

Czapicka, John. "Lemberg, Leopolis, Lwów, Lvov: A City in the Crosscurrents of European Culture." In idem, *Lviv: A City in the Crosscurrents of Culture.* Harvard Ukrainian Studies, vol. xxiv. Cambridge: Ukrainian Research Institute, 2000.

Davies, Norman. *God's Playground: A History of Poland,* vol. 1. New York: Columbia University Press, 1982.

Davis, Joseph. "The 'Ten Questions' of Eliezer Eilburg and the Problem of Jewish Unbelief in the 16th Century," *Jewish Quarterly Review* 91 (3–4) 2001, 293–336.

Dembitzer, Hayyim Natan, *Kelilat yofi: Kolel toldot ha-rabanim be-'ir Lvov*. Reprint New York: Zeev, 1959.

Ismar Elbogen, *Jewish Liturgy : A Comprehensive History*. Philadelphia : Jewish Publication Society. New York: Jewish Theological Seminary of America, 1993.

Ellenson, David. *Rabbi Esriel Hildesheimer and the Creation of a Modern Jewish Orthodoxy*. Tuscaloosa: University Alabama Press, 2003.

Eshcoly, A. Z. "Rezah Harav Avraham Kohn z'l," *Davar* 11.6.1934, 6.

Friedman, Filip. *Die galizischen Juden in Kampfe um ihre Gleichberechtigung (1848–1868)*. Frankfurt am Main: Kaufmann Verlag, 1929.

Gartner, Haim. "Rabanut ve-dayanut be-Galitsiyah be-mahazit ha-rishonah shel ha-meah ha-19: Tipologiyah shel hanhagah mesoratit be-mashber," unpublished Ph.D. dissertation, Hebrew University of Jerusalem, 2004.

Gelber, N. M. ed., *Lvov*. Jerusalem and Tel-Aviv: Enziklopediah shel galuyot, 1956.

Guterman, Alexander. "The Origins of the Great Synagogue in Warsaw on Tłomackie. Street," in W. T. Bartoszewski and Antony Polonsky, *The Jews in Warsaw*. Oxford: Oxford University Press, 1991, 181–210.

Halevi, David. *Rezah be-yerushalayim*. Jerusalem: Tefuzah, 1983.

Hirsch, Samson Raphael. *Nineteen Letters*. Jerusalem and New York: Feldheim Publishers, 1995.

Hrytsak, Yaroslav. "Lviv: A Multicultural History through the Centuries," in John Czapicka, ed., *Lviv: A City in the Crosscurrents of Culture*. Harvard Ukrainian Studies, vol. xxiv. Cambridge: Ukrainian Research Institute, 2000.

Katz, Jacob, *Tradition and Crisis: Jewish Society at the End of the Middle Ages*, Translated and with an afterword and bibliography by Bernard Cooperman. New York : New York University Press, 1993.

Karl, Zvi, "Lvov," *Arim ve-imahot be-yisrael*, vol. 1. Jerusalem: Mosad Harav Kook, 1946.

Karl, Zvi. "Hayim datiim shel yehudei Lvov," *Entsiklopediah shel galuyot*, vol. 4. Jerusalem-Tel Aviv, 1956.

Kohn, Gotthilf. *Abraham Kohn im Lichte der Geschichtsforschung: historische Studie verfasst zum 50-sten Gedenkjahre des Todes des Rabbiners*. Zamarstynow bei Lemberg: Im Selbstverlage des Verfassers, 1898.

Kohn, Jakob. *Leben und Wirken Abraham Kohns*. Lemberg: Poremba, 1855.

Landau, Moshe (M.Lan) "Lvov," *Encyclopedia Judaica*. Jerusalem: Keter, 1972, vol. 10.

Lowenstein, Steven. *The Berlin Jewish Community: Enlightenment, Family, and Crisis, 1770–1830*. New York: Oxford University Press, 1994.

Magocsi, Paul R. *Galicia: A Historical Survey and Bibliographic Guide*. Toronto: University of Toronto Press, 1983.

Mahler, Raphael. *Hasidism and the Jewish Enlightenment: Their Confrontation in Galicia and Poland in the First Half of the Nineteenth Century*, translated from the Yiddish by Eugene Orenstein; translated from the Hebrew by Aaron Klein and Jenny Machlowitz Klein. Philadelphia: Jewish Publication Society of America, 1985.

McCagg, William O. *A History of Habsburg Jews, 1670–1918*. Bloomington: Indiana University Press, 1989.

Margaliot, Reuven. "Rabanim verashei-yeshivot," in Gelber, N.M. ed., *Lvov*. Jerusalem and Tel-Aviv: Enziklopediah shel galuyot, 1956, vol. 4.

Mendelssohn, Moses. *Jerusalem*, translated Alan Arkush. Waltham: Brandeis University Press, 1983.

Meyer, Michael. "Religious Reform," in *The YIVO Encyclopedia of Jews in Eastern Europe*. http://www.yivo.org.

Meyer, Michael. *Response to Modernity: A History of the Reform Movement in Judaism*. New York: Oxford University Press, 1988.

Moshe-Zahav, Zvi and Meshi-Zahav, Yehudah. *Ha-qadosh: Rabi Ya'aqov Yisrael DeHaan*. Jerusalem: Mahon hayahadut haharedit, 1996.

Nakdimon, Shlomo and Mayzlish, Shaul. *DeHaan: Ha-rezah hapoliti harishon beerez yisrael*. Tel Aviv: Modan, 1985.

Nedavah, Yosef, ed. *Ha-neesham ha-sheni: maavako shel Tsevi Rozenblat le-gilui haemet*. Tel-Aviv: Jabotinsky Institute, 1986.

Peltz, Diana. "Central State Historical Archives of Ukraine in L'viv," http://www.rtrfoundation.org/webart/UkraineChapters-Peltz.pdf.

Rubinstein, Shimon. *Shmonim shanah lehahlatat bet ha-din hasodi hameyuhad shel ha-"Haganah" ladun lemavet et Yaakov De-Haan*. Jerusalem: private offprint, 2004.

Scholem, Gershom. "Redemption through Sin," in his *The Messianic Idea in Judaism*. New York: Schocken Books, 1995, 78–141.

Schorsch, Ismar. "Emancipation and the Crisis of Religious Authority: The Emergence of the Modern Rabbinate," in Werner Mosse et al. eds., *Revolution and Evolution: 1848 in German-Jewish History*. Tübingen: Mohr, 1981, 205–248.

Shmeruk, Khone. "Mashma'auta ha-hevratit shel hashehitah hehasidit," *Mehkarim betoldot yisrael ba'et hahadashah* 1 (1995), 161–186.

Silber, Michael. "The Emergence of Ultra-Orthodoxy; the Invention of a Tradition," in Jack Wertheimer, ed., *The Uses of Tradition*. New York: Jewish Theological Seminary of America 199, 23–84.

Sinkoff, Nancy. *Out of the Shtetl: Making Jews Modern in the Polish Borderlands*. Providence: Brown Judaic Studies, 2004.

Spinoza, Benedict. *Theological-Political Treatise*, translated by R. Elwes. Indianapolis: Hackett, 2001.

Stanislawski, Michael. *Autobiographical Jews: Essays in Jewish Self-Fashioning*. Seattle: University of Washington Press, 2004.

Stanislawski, Michael. "Reflections on the Russian Rabbinate," in Jack Wertheimer, ed., *Jewish Religious Leadership: Image and Reality*. New York: Jewish Theological Seminary, 2004, vol. 1, 429–446.

Stanislawski, Michael, *Tsar Nicholas I and the Jews: The Transformation of Jewish Society in Russia, 1825–1855*. Philadelphia: The Jewish Publication Society, 1983.

Stanislawski, Michael. *Zionism and the Fin de Siècle*. Berkeley: University of California Press, 2003.

Suchestow, Gawril. *Mazevet qodesh: Hu zikhron zadikim, sefer zikaron lekhol hageonim vehaqedoshim bevet mo'ed lekhol hai po 'ir L'vov*. Lemberg: Matfes, 1863.

Tänzer, Aron. *Die Geschichte der Juden in Hohenems*. Bregenz: Lingenhöle, 1982.

Teter, Magda. *Jews and Heretics in Catholic Poland: A Beleaguered Church in the Post-Reformation Era*. New York: Cambridge University Press, 2006.

Tevet, Shabtai. *Rezah Arlozorov*. Jerusalem: Schocken, 1982.

Wandycz, Piotr. *The Lands of Partitioned Poland, 1795–1918*. University of Washington Press: Seattle, 1974.

Wierzbienic, Waclaw. "The Processes of Jewish Emancipation and Assimilation in the Multiethnic City of Lviv during the Nineteenth and Twentieth Centuries," in Czaplicka, John, *Lviv: A City in the Crosscurrents of Culture*. Harvard Ukrainian Studies, vol. xxiv. Cambridge: Ukrainian Research Institute, 2000, 223–250.

Index